Exploring the
Planets!

The Latest Information and Out-of-This-World
Activities That Teach Kids About the Wonders
And Workings of the Solar System

Astronaut in space

Planet Mars

Man on the Moon

by Bonnie Sachatello-Sawyer

SCHOLASTIC
PROFESSIONAL BOOKS

New York • Toronto • London • Auckland • Sydney • Mexico City • New Delhi • Hong Kong

dedication

FOR MY STAR—JOSEPH EDWARD SAWYER

acknowledgments

This book would not be possible without the expertise and assistance of many talented people, including: Sandra Bellingham, Duncan Bullock, Marianne Hansen, Karen Kellaher, Jim Manning, Linda Martel, Dr. Judith Meyer, Mike Murray, Dr. Meredith Olson, Jeff Taylor, Dr. Neil de Grasse Tyson, Walt Woolbaugh, Dr. Gregory Vogt, and Sue Winstead.

Rocketing Toward Planets activity adapted from *Rockets: A Teacher's Guide With Activities in Science, Mathematics and Technology* by NASA Education Working Group (1996 NASA publication EG-1996-09-108-HQ).

Mega Martian Volcanoes adapted from *Generalizing Volcanoes From Earth to Mars* by Dr. Meredith Olson, Jet Propulsion Laboratory, NASA.

Moving on Mars activity adapted from *Planetary Rovers* by Dr. Meredith Olson, Jet Propulsion Laboratory, NASA.

We Are the Planets play by Sandra Bellingham.

Photograph Sources: National Space Science Data Center, NASA.

Cover and interior design: Holly Grundon

Photographic Sources: National Space Science Data Center, NASA

ISBN: 0-590-68573-2

Contents

CHAPTER ONE — PLANET BASICS

Background Information 6
Frequently Asked Questions 7

Activities

.............K-W-L Chart 9
.............Planet Mobiles 10
.............Planet Mini-Book 11
.............Looking at Planets 12
.............Observing Planets at Night 13
.............Planet Orbits 14
.............Tracking Planets 15
.............Create a Mnemonic Device 15
.............Modern Planet Poetry 15
.............The Age of the Solar System 15
.............What's in a Name? 16
.............Solar System Diagram (Poster Activity) 16

CHAPTER TWO — THE ROCKY PLANETS

Background Information 28

.............Mercury 28
.............Venus 29
.............Earth 30
.............Mars 31
.............Frequently Asked Questions 32

Activities

Readers' Theater:

The Rocky Planet Weather Report 34
Comparing Mercury and the Moon 34
Exploring the Blue Planet 34
Mapping Earth's Continents 35
Mars Ice Caps 36
Mega Martian Volcanoes 37
Model a Martian Landscape 38

CONTINUED ON NEXT PAGE

Contents

CHAPTER THREE | THE GAS PLANETS AND PLUTO

Background Information 44
.... Jupiter 44
.... Saturn 45
.... Uranus 46
.... Neptune 47
.... Pluto 47
.... Frequently Asked Questions 48

Activities
.... Readers' Theater: The Gas Planet Weather Report 49
.... Puzzling Pluto 49
.... Great Planetary Graph 49
.... Design Your Own Minor Planet 49
.... Picture Jupiter 49
.... Mini-Book: Saturn's Ears 50
.... Calculate Your Weight on Earth, Jupiter, and Pluto ... 50
.... Comparing Gases 50
.... Neptune's Spinning Rings 50

CHAPTER FOUR | VISITING THE PLANETS

Background Information 60
Frequently Asked Questions 62

Activities
.... Play: We Are the Planets 64
.... Poem: Star Gazers 64
.... Rockets Away 65
.... Design a Planet Rover 66

Mission to Mars 67
Sketch a Stamp 67
Video Visions of Planets 67
Show What You Know 67
Party on, Planets 67
Suggested Classroom Resources 78
Answer Key 80

Dear Teacher,

Do you remember where you were the first time you saw a planet or really looked at the night sky? Many of us have cherished memories of such moments. Our fascination with the sky is part of our insatiable human need to learn about the natural world. And children are certainly no exception. As you know from experience, youngsters are forever asking questions about the universe around them. This book will help you provide some answers based on the latest planetary discoveries and expert opinions.

This book is intended as a thorough and exciting theme unit on the planets. You can select from a number of fascinating introductory activities in the first chapter, then focus on the individual planets that make up our solar system by choosing activities from chapters 2 and 3. You'll find facts and fun related to the rocky planets (Mercury, Venus, Earth, and Mars) in chapter 2, and loads of information on the giant gas planets (Jupiter, Saturn, Uranus, and Neptune) plus Pluto in chapter 3. Chapter 4 wraps up your unit by providing a glimpse at how humans explore the new frontiers of space, including solar systems beyond our own.

One of the most important activities you'll encounter in the book is observing the planets at night. Nothing can rival the thrill of seeing a planet or moon through the lens of a telescope on a clear night. While the logistics of organizing an evening sky-observation experience for your class may be complicated, the experience is well worth it. Many of your students will recall the experience for a lifetime. I also highly recommend that you involve parents in your study of planets. Encourage them to look at the night sky with their children. You—and they—may be amazed at what they discover together.

As I wrote this book in my Montana home, I watched Venus appear above the Elkhorn Mountains each night. The familiar light inspired me along the way. I hope you will find the information and activities useful and engaging as you take your own journey through the solar system.

Sincerely,

Bonnie Sachatello-Sawyer

Dr. Bonnie Sachatello-Sawyer
Division Head for Programs
Museum of the Rockies

Background Information

Planet Temperatures

All temperatures are given in Fahrenheit.

Mercury
270° below zero to 800°

Venus
900°

Earth
60° below zero to 130°

Mars
185° below zero to 77°

Jupiter
180° below zero

Saturn
292° below zero

Uranus
366° below zero

Neptune
357° below zero

Pluto
378° below zero

Did You Know?

The word *planet* comes from the Greek word *planetes asteres,* which means "wandering stars." Why did the ancient Greeks think the planets were "wandering"? As the planets move around the Sun, we see them in different places each night.

O ur solar system is made up of the Sun and everything that moves around it. This system includes our Sun, the planets, moons, asteroids, comets, meteors—even tiny space dust. The planets and other objects are in constant motion, fueled by energy from the Sun. They have captured the human imagination for thousands of years and continue to do so today.

Planets are spinning bodies of rock and gas that orbit around a star. Unlike stars, planets do not give off any light of their own. Instead, they reflect the light of the star around which they revolve.

In our solar system, there are nine major planets—Mercury, Venus, Earth, Mars, Jupiter, Saturn, Uranus, Neptune, and Pluto—as well as thousands of minor planets or "asteroids." Both the major and minor planets circle around one star—the Sun. The Sun's strong gravitational pull keeps the planets and asteroids moving around it.

From planet Earth, we can see some of the other planets almost every night. They are often the first bright starlike objects we see in the sky right after sunset.

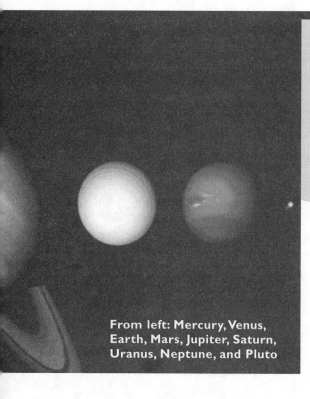

Did You Know?

Some ancient rock art has been linked to planets. Venus was often drawn as a great star.

Frequently Asked Questions

Who Discovered the Planets?

People have gazed at planets in wonder for centuries. The ancient Greeks and Romans knew Mercury, Venus, Mars, Jupiter, and Saturn existed. They named these planets after their gods of speed, love, war, kings, and time, respectively. Much later, with the aid of a telescope, Uranus was discovered. It was first spotted in 1781 by Sir William Herschel. In 1846, Neptune was found when mathematicians noticed this planet's gravitational pull on Uranus. Pluto was discovered in 1930 by astronomer Clyde Tombaugh.

Humans at first just imagined what these other worlds were like. We dreamed of Martians and spaceships. In the past 40 years, however, scientists have used spacecraft, radar, satellites, cameras, and computers to learn more about the solar system. Advances in technology have provided new understandings about planets, how the solar system formed, and what the future might hold.

Fast Facts About Planets

Planet	Average Distance from Sun	Diameter	Moons	Rings	Type
Mercury	36 million miles	3,010 miles	0	no	rock
Venus	67 million miles	7,520 miles	0	no	rock
Earth	93 million miles	7,926 miles	1	no	rock
Mars	142 million miles	4,220 miles	2	no	rock
Jupiter	483 million miles	88,800 miles	16	yes	gas
Saturn	885 million miles	74,000 miles	18	yes	gas
Uranus	1,780 million miles	31,750 miles	18	yes	gas
Neptune	2,800 million miles	27,200 miles	8	yes	gas
Pluto	3,600 million miles	1,420 miles	1	no	ice/rock

Who Studies Planets?

Geologists
Astronomers
Chemists

Mathematicians
Physicists
Biologists

Meteorologists
Planetarium Directors
Astronauts

? Frequently Asked Questions

Using space telescopes and other new technology, scientists have been able to photograph the formation of a new planet (shown here).

Where Did Planets Come From?

Current scientific evidence suggests that all objects in our solar system, including the Sun, planets, moons, asteroids, meteoroids, and comets, formed out of a huge cloud of gas, rock, and dust called a nebula about 5 billion years ago.

The outer planets, Jupiter, Saturn, Uranus, Neptune, and Pluto, formed primarily from gas, ice, and space dust in the giant nebula. The inner planets, Mercury, Venus, Earth, and Mars, formed from clumps of rock. Moons also formed around most of the planets.

Scientists know there are more planets outside of our solar system. Using very powerful telescopes, astronomers can see disks of dust and gas around young stars. Astronomers have also detected the presence of Jupiter-like planets around some stars as a result of the gravitational tugs they exert on their parent stars.

Why Do Some Planets Have Moons?

Most planets have moons (also called "satellites") that are made of ice, rock, and frozen gas. They orbit around planets just as planets orbit around the Sun. Each moon also spins on its own axis. Amazingly, no two moons are exactly alike. For example:

- One of Mars's moons, called Phobos, is relatively small and potato-shaped, with dark carbon-rich rock. Some experts believe Phobos may once have been an asteroid that was captured by Mars's gravitational field.

- Jupiter has several interesting moons. One of them, called Io, has active volcanoes which spew sulfur, oxygen, and sodium into space. Another, called Europa, is covered in a thin crust of ice and may have an ocean of water hidden beneath its crust. Jupiter's Ganymede moon is covered in deep cracks—probably the result of the moon's crust once having broken apart.

- Neptune's largest moon, Triton, has geysers that release nitrogen gas into the atmosphere. Triton also moves around its planet backward—that is, in the opposite direction of the planet's rotation.

K-W-L Chart

This learning tool is the perfect springboard to the study of planets because it gives kids the opportunity to tap prior knowledge and choose the subtopics they want to know more about.

A K-W-L CHART:

K: Kids tell what they **know**.

W: Kids tell what they **want** to know.

L: Kids tell what they've **learned**.

It will help ensure that your planet unit is learner-centered and exciting!

What we know about planets	What we want to know about planets	What we have learned about planets

MATERIALS:

● planet shapes copied onto red, green, and blue paper (use the outlines of Jupiter and Saturn on page 23 if you'd like)

● masking tape

At the close of your unit, revisit the K-W-L chart by asking students to help you read each planet fact. You'll be amazed at what the class has learned!

DIRECTIONS:

1 Use masking tape to divide a large wall space into three columns (making the third column about twice as large as each of the other two). Label the first "What we know about planets"; label the second "What we want to know about planets"; label the third "What we have learned about planets."

2 Invite kids to brainstorm facts they already know about planets, such as "Planets orbit around the Sun" or "There are nine planets, including Earth." Record each fact on a blue planet shape. (See page 17 for a reproducible pattern.) Tape them in the first column.

3 Invite students to brainstorm questions they would like to have answered, such as "Which is the biggest planet?" or "Who discovered the planets?" Record each question on a green planet shape and tape it in the second column.

4 Now it's time to get cracking at the answers to those intriguing questions. Over the course of the unit, each time the class finds out an answer, write—or have students write—the new fact on a red planet shape and hang it in the "What we have learned" column. (The facts you add to the third column need not be limited to the questions asked.)

Planet Mobiles

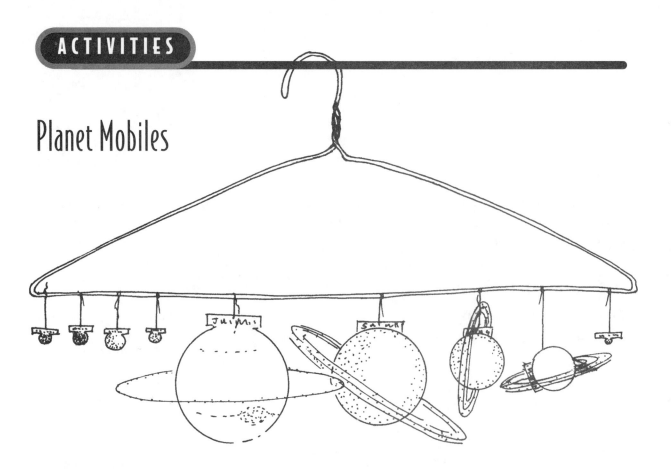

To get students thinking about the different planets and their order around the Sun, help students make their own planet mobiles. Students can either create complete mobiles as an introductory activity or add individual planets to their mobiles as the class studies them.

MATERIALS:

- coat hangers
- string (9 one-foot-long pieces per child)
- hole punch
- scissors
- crayons or markers
- copies of the reproducible found on page 23

DIRECTIONS:

1 Display the solar system poster that came with this book as a visual reference.

2 Distribute the supplies and hang up a model of one of the planet mobiles already assembled so students understand how to put one together.

3 Invite students to cut out the reproducible planet pieces along the dotted lines.

4 Encourage your students to color each of the planets, then lay them out in the order of their distance from the Sun. (For the purposes of this activity, do not worry about trying to keep the distances between the planets proportional.) Children may wish to add interesting, accurate features, such as moons or spots. While students are coloring, walk around and help each child punch holes in each of the pieces.

5 Next, distribute nine pieces of string to each child. Demonstrate how to thread each piece of string through a hole in a planet piece and then knot it. Tie the other end onto the hanger.

6 When the mobiles are complete, invite students to share their mobiles with one another. Hang the mobiles in your classroom while you continue your planets unit.

Planet Mini-Book

DIRECTIONS:

As students learn about the planets, encourage them to record their newfound knowledge in their very own mini-books. Each page of the mini-book instructs students to jot down a planet's distance from the Sun, color, moons, rings, and other interesting facts. The book serves as an excellent way to assess student learning. To assemble the books:

1 Copy the reproducible on pages 17–18, 19–20, and 21–22 on standard 8.5 x 11 inch paper. Make the pages double-sided.

2 Fold the front cover/back cover in half along the dotted line.

3 Fold each inner page in half, keeping the fold to the right side.

4 Place the inner pages inside the cover, keeping the page numbers in correct order. Staple the edge to bind the book.

5 Have students add facts and planet illustrations.

Note: Students will find facts and pictures to help them make their mini-books on the poster that came with this book. They can also log on to one of the helpful Web sites listed on page 78.

Looking at Planets

Set up an activity station to help students learn how to focus binoculars to observe planets.

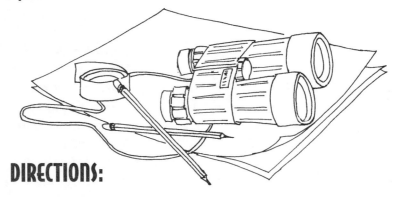

MATERIALS:

- 2 to 3 pairs of binoculars
- tape
- ladder or chair
- blank paper and pencils
- small pictures of the planets (see page 13)
- poster of the planets that accompanied this book

DIRECTIONS:

1 Before class, make a photocopy of the four small planet pictures on page 13. Cut the planet pictures apart and tape a copy of each picture onto one of your classroom walls near the ceiling. (You may need a ladder or chair to stand on.) Place the planet pictures about two feet apart. Be sure to put the planet pictures on a wall that has no windows.

2 Have students stand on the opposite side of the classroom from where the planet images are located. Introduce the binoculars and demonstrate how to use them to find the "planet" pictures. Help each of your kids locate a planet with the aid of the binoculars.

3 Once students have found a planet, encourage them to trace what they see on a piece of paper and then identify the planet using the enclosed poster.

Extensions

1 Try coloring these planet pictures with glow-in-the-dark markers. Then turn off the lights and let students find them with their binoculars.

2 Cover a set of the planet patterns (page 23) in foil. Pass them out to nine of your students and have kids point them toward the center of the room. Then turn off the lights and turn on a small flashlight in the center of the room to represent the Sun. Discuss with your students the fact that planets do not give off light of their own, but instead reflect light from the Sun.

Mars

Jupiter

Saturn

Uranus

Once students have mastered using binoculars indoors, it is easier to help them see the real planets using binoculars at night.

Observing Planets at Night

MATERIALS:

● sky map (see directions)

● binoculars or telescope

DIRECTIONS:

1 Spark your kids' interest by having them observe the planets at night as a homework assignment. To find out what planets are currently visible, look for a recent sky map in *Astronomy* or *Sky and Telescope* magazine or log on to the following Web site: **http://www.calweb.com/`mcharvey/.**
A current sky map will show in what direction to look and in what constellation a planet will appear to be in. Using the sky map as a guide, students can go outside, locate the constellation, then look for the planet. You will not observe planets moving in just one night. They will instead appear as fixed starlike objects. But if you can observe planets over time, you will find they move through a band of 12 constellations known as the zodiac. The constellations or "star patterns" that make up the zodiac include Aquarius, Pisces, Aries, Taurus, Gemini, Cancer, Leo, Virgo, Libra, Scorpius, Sagittarius, and Capricornus.

2 Call your local planetarium or astronomical society and ask it to help you arrange an evening telescope observation session for your students. You may also want to write a note to all students' parents encouraging them to take their children outside to observe planets after dark.

TIPS In addition to using a sky map, keep in mind the following.

Using Your Eyes:
Venus: can usually be seen before sunrise or right after sunset.
Mars: can be seen best when the Earth is between the Sun and Mars. This happens approximately every 25 months.
Jupiter: can be seen sometime during the night for most of the year.
Saturn: the most distant planet you can see without a telescope.

Using a Telescope:
Jupiter: look for some of its moons.
Saturn: look for its rings.

Planet Orbits

Most planet orbits are almost circular. Because they are not perfectly round, however, they are considered to be ellipses. To help students understand orbits, head out to the playground for a fun, hands-on activity.

MATERIALS:

- signs that read Sun, Mercury, Venus, Earth, etc.

- a watch with a second hand

DIRECTIONS:

1 Go outdoors. Appoint one student to be the Sun. Appoint nine others to be the planets. Give each of the "planets" a sign with the planet name on it.

2 Encourage Mercury to walk slowly around in a counterclockwise circle around the Sun.

3 Invite Venus to walk in a larger counterclockwise circle around Mercury's orbit.

4 Have each of the remaining students representing planets, (i.e., Earth, Mars...) walk in progressively larger circles around the Sun. Once your students have a better idea of how planets move around the Sun, have them line up near each other (about an arm's length apart).

5 When everyone is in position, tell students they should take a single normal-size step in their orbits every time you say "step." While they are walking, each "planet" should keep track of the number of times it circles the Sun. Time them doing this activity for two minutes.

6 Invite each "planet" to share the number of times it walks around the Sun in the two-minute time period. Based on this information, which planet has the longest year? (Pluto) Which has the shortest year? (Mercury) Explain that this is the concept of revolution (the motion of one object around another; one revolution around the Sun equals a planet's "year").

Rotation Demonstration

7 Have one of the planets spin in place. Introduce the concept of rotation (the spinning of an object about an internal axis: one rotation equals a planet's "day").

8 See if students can spin around and move in a circle at the same time, simulating a planet's rotation and revolution. Remember that the Sun also spins on its own axis.

Tracking Planets

Using the reproducible found on page 24 and scissors, help students understand that as planets orbit around the Sun, they appear to move around the sky.

Create a Mnemonic Device!

Use the activity on page 25 to help students create their own tricks for remembering the order of the planets.

Modern Planet Poetry

Share the following contemporary poem with students. Then inspire your students to write a poem of their own based on a planet theme.

Many Moons

Though Venus has none, Earth has one ...
And Jupiter has sixteen!
Yes, many a planet has moons around it.
Whatever does this mean?

A moon is a planet's faithful pal.
Around the planet it goes.
A moon can be made of rock, ice, or gas,
As any astronomer knows.

From Phobos to Europa,
Each moon is given a name.
Moons come in many sizes —
No two are exactly the same!

—Karen Kellaher

The Age of the Solar System

Scientists believe that Earth is about 4.6 billion years old (other planets in our solar system are probably similar in age). That's 4,600 million years old—or 4,600,000,000 birthdays! It's hard for anyone to imagine that much time. To get your students thinking about the amount of time that has lapsed since the Earth and other planets were formed, try this short activity with them.

MATERIALS:

● watch or clock with a second hand, or stopwatch

DIRECTIONS:

1 Instruct students to close their eyes and put their heads down on their desks. Tell them to keep their head down until they think one minute has passed. When they think a minute has passed, have them quietly raise their heads.

2 Announce a "start" when students should be mentally calculating their own sense of a minute (and you start watching a clock). Announce when the minute is up. How well did students do? Ask your students how they decided when a minute had passed.

3 Try the same experiment for three minutes. Discuss the difficulty in imagining 4.6 billion years when we have trouble even calculating the length of a minute.

Did You Know?

If you stacked one piece of paper on top of another for each year of Earth's history, you would have a stack of paper $3^{1}/_{2}$ miles high!

What's in a Name?

Using the activity found on page 26, challenge students to match each planet to its Greek or Roman name.

Extension

Play portions of "The Planets" by Gustav Holst (many recordings are available). This classical music suite, written from 1914 to 1916, was based on the astrological and mythological aspects of the planets. Based on the music, invite your students to draw the environments of each of these planets.

POSTER ACTIVITY

Solar System Diagram

As you have probably already discovered, the colorful solar system map that came with this book makes an excellent tool for teaching and learning about the planets. Hang the poster in a prominent spot in your classroom, and call students' attention to it whenever they need to remember the location, appearance, or order of the planets. You can also create an exciting scavenger–hunt game using your poster. Divide students into teams of three or four, then distribute a photocopy of the Scavenger Hunt reproducible (page 27) to each team. Give each group a few minutes to look closely at the poster and complete the scavenger–hunt form. Award a prize to the team or teams which gets all ten responses correct.

ld Here

My Name _____

My Book of the

Planets

Pluto

How far from the Sun? _____

How many moons? _____

Does it have rings? _____

What color is it? _____

Another fun fact about Pluto is _____
_____

Neptune

How far from the Sun? _____

How many moons? _____

Does it have rings? _____

What color is it? _____

Another fun fact about **Neptune** is _____

---

old Here

Mercury

How far from the Sun? _____

How many moons? _____

Does it have rings? _____

What color is it? _____

Another fun fact about **Mercury** is _____

Uranus

How far from the Sun? _____

How many moons? _____

Does it have rings? _____

What color is it? _____

Another fun fact about Uranus is _____
_____

Venus

How far from the Sun? _____

How many moons? _____

Does it have rings? _____

What color is it? _____

Another fun fact about Venus is _____
_____

Saturn

How far from the Sun? _____

How many moons? _____

Does it have rings? _____

What color is it? _____

Another fun fact about Saturn is _____

_____

_____

---

old Here

Earth

How far from the Sun? _____

How many moons? _____

Does it have rings? _____

What color is it? _____

Another fun fact about Earth is _____

_____

_____

Jupiter

How far from the Sun? _____

How many moons? _____

Does it have rings? _____

What color is it? _____

Another fun fact about Jupiter is _____

⑦

Fold Here

Mars

How far from the Sun? _____

How many moons? _____

Does it have rings? _____

What color is it? _____

Another fun fact about Mars is _____

⑥

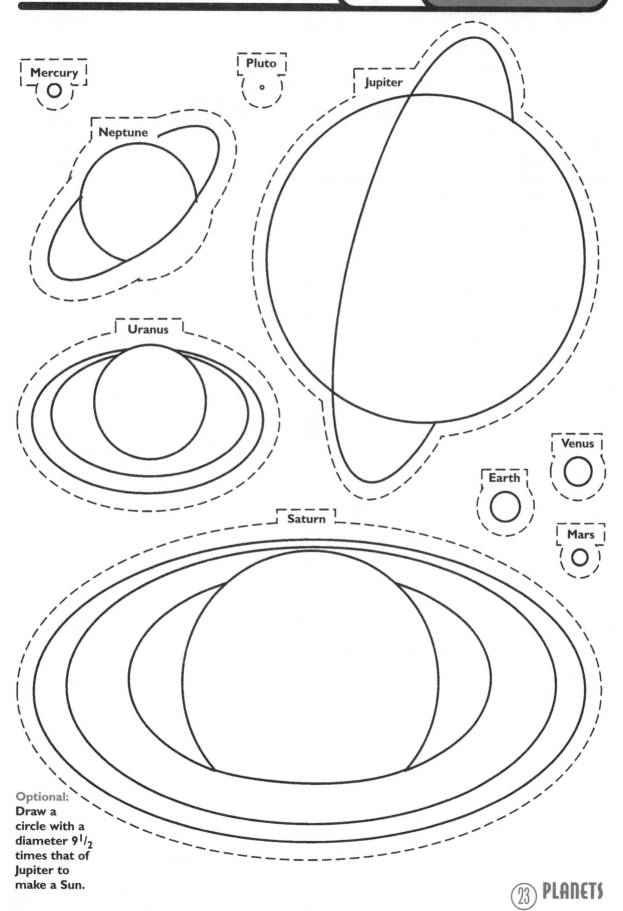

Mercury

Pluto

Jupiter

Neptune

Uranus

Venus

Earth

Mars

Saturn

Optional:
Draw a
circle with a
diameter $9\frac{1}{2}$
times that of
Jupiter to
make a Sun.

Name_____

Tracking Planets

Most planets move west to east. They appear to wander through constellations. Cut apart each of the pictures of Mars (represented by an ◯) in the constellation Sagittarius and see if you can put them in the correct order.

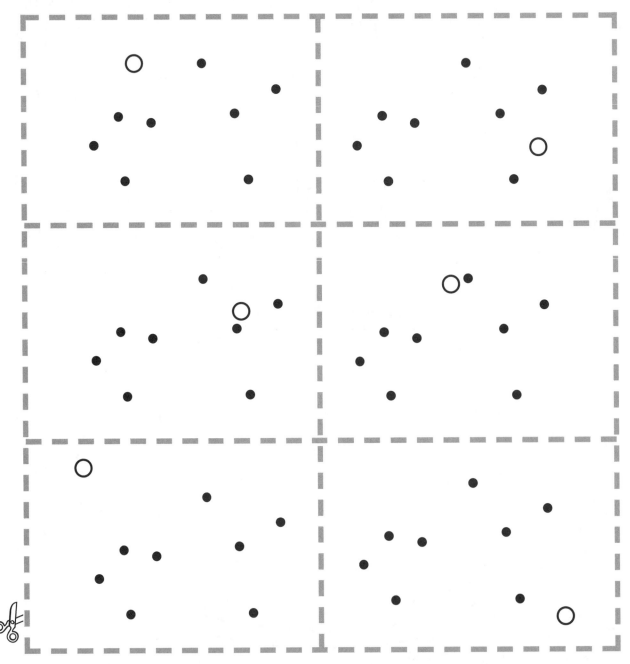

Name _____

Order the Planets

A mnemonic device can help you remember something.
It uses the first letter of each word.

Here's one mnemonic phrase to help you
remember the order of the planets.

Mercury	**M**y
Venus	**V**ery
Earth	**E**xtraordinary
Mars	**M**om
Jupiter	**J**ust
Saturn	**S**at
Uranus	**U**pon
Neptune	**N**ine
Pluto	**P**orcupines

Can you create others?

M _____	**M** _____
V _____	**V** _____
E _____	**E** _____
M _____	**M** _____
J _____	**J** _____
S _____	**S** _____
U _____	**U** _____
N _____	**N** _____
P _____	**P** _____

Name _____

What's in a Name?

The ancient Greeks and Romans spotted Mercury, Venus, Mars, Jupiter, and Saturn. They named these planets for gods and goddesses. Can you match each planet with the god or goddess that it is named after? Cut out the five planet stamps at the bottom. Then, paste each one in the correct box below. If you get stumped, use the *Our Solar System* poster as a guide.

CLUE
This planet was linked with the god of time because it took nearly 30 years to circle the Sun. It is famous for its many rings.

CLUE
This red planet reminded ancient astronomers of the Roman god of war.

CLUE
Named for the Swift-footed messenger of the Roman gods, this planet moves around the Sun faster than the other planets do.

CLUE
The largest of all the planets, this striped planet was named for the Roman king of all the gods and goddesses.

CLUE
This planet was named after the Roman goddess of love. It is second from the Sun.

Venus

Mercury

Jupiter

Mars

Saturn

Team Members _____

Solar System Scavenger Hunt

Use your classroom poster of the planets to find each item on the list!

1. A planet with rings _____

2. The second planet from the Sun _____

3. The smallest planet _____

4. A planet that is more than 2 billion miles from the Sun

_____

5. A planet that is less than 50 million miles from the Sun

_____

6. The closest planet to Pluto _____

7. The color of Mars _____

8. A planet with an unusual-shaped orbit _____

9. The planet closest to Earth _____

10. The star which all the planets orbit around _____

Background Information

The Rocky Planets

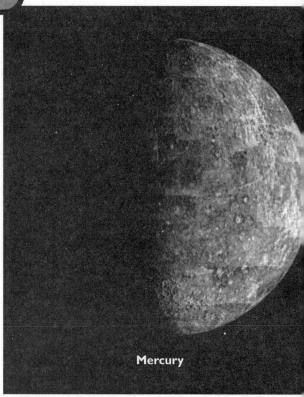

Mercury

Mercury, Venus, Earth, and Mars are commonly called the "rocky planets." They are the four planets closest to the Sun and share a few features in common. All have a solid surface and a core made of heavy metals. All of these planets except Mercury have a significant atmosphere—a blanket of gases which surrounds them. None of these planets has rings.

Mercury

Color: gray

Size: 3,031 miles across

Distance from Sun: 36 million miles

Moons: 0

Rings: none

Day (one spin): 59 Earth days

Year (a trip around the Sun): 88 Earth days

Orbiting speed: 30 miles per second

Gravity: An 85-pound child would weigh 32 pounds.

Mercury is the planet closest to the Sun. It is about one third the diameter of Earth and has no moons of its own. Like the Earth's Moon, Mercury has lots of meteor craters and flat plains covered by a powdery soil. It's also dry and has only a thin sodium cloud for an atmosphere. Mercury's core is thought to be made of iron because Mercury is as dense as Earth even though the planet is much smaller.

A spacecraft called Mariner 10 flew by Mercury in 1974–75 and took pictures of about half the planet. The pictures revealed that Mercury has a lot of hills and cracks—a result both of the planet shrinking early in its formation and of numerous impacts with meteorites and other space objects.

From Earth, Mercury is difficult to see because it is so close to the Sun. The Sun's light obscures it from our view. Sky watchers are most likely to glimpse Mercury in the spring right after the Sun sets or in the fall just before dawn.

Venus

Earth

Mars

Venus

Color: yellow-white

Size: 7,521 miles across

Distance from Sun: 67 million miles

Moons: 0

Rings: none

Day (one spin):
243 Earth days

Year (a trip around the Sun):
225 Earth days

Orbiting speed:
22 miles per second

Gravity: An 85-pound child would weigh 77 pounds.

Venus is the planet closest to Earth, and while it is similar in size, density, and gravitational pull, it is physically very different. Covered in clouds and haze made of sulfuric acid, Venus's surface is hidden from view. The atmosphere is about 98 percent carbon dioxide. The carbon dioxide traps the Sun's heat so that Venus is hot (up to 900 degrees Fahrenheit) both day and night. Venus rotates in the opposite direction of the other planets, so the Sun rises in the west and sets in the east. Because Venus orbits the Sun faster than it rotates on its own axis, a day on Venus is longer than its year!

Much of the information we have about Venus came from NASA's Pioneer Venus spacecraft mission in 1978, the Magellan radar-mapping mission in 1990, and several Soviet missions. Information has also been collected from Earth-based radar telescopes and imaging systems. These efforts have provided detailed panoramas of Venus, topographical maps, and even chemical analysis for the planet's surface rocks. Radar has revealed that Venus has large lava plains and thousands of inactive volcanoes and mountains, but fewer craters than Earth's Moon or Mercury.

From Earth, Venus can be seen as much as three hours before sunrise or after sunset. Venus is the third-brightest object visible in the sky after the Sun and Earth's moon.

Did You Know?

Almost all of the features on Venus are named after famous women. Three main craters are named after Anna Pavlova (prima ballerina, c. 1881-1931), Sacagawea (Shoshone Indian who traveled with Lewis and Clark, c. 1789-1812), and Sappho (Greek poet, circa 610-580 B.C.).

Earth

Did You Know?

U.S. astronaut Neil Armstrong was the first person to walk on Earth's Moon. On July 21, 1969, he took the famous step and remarked, "That's one small step for man, one giant leap for mankind."

Color:
blue and white

Size:
7,926 miles across

Distance from Sun:
93 million miles

Moons: 1

Rings: none

Day (one spin):
24 hours

Year (a trip around the Sun):
365.25 Earth days

Orbiting speed:
19 miles per second

Gravity:
An 85-pound child weighs 85 pounds.

Earth is the only planet that we know of with water in three forms: liquid, ice, and gas (water vapor). Water is found in Earth's hospitable oceans, on continents, and in the atmosphere. The abundance of water on Earth has enabled many life-forms to flourish—including us! While water sustains all living things, Earth's oxygen and nitrogen atmosphere protects us from the harmful rays of the Sun. The atmosphere and the oceans also spread heat from the Sun around the planet, creating milder climates that can support life.

Earth is a constantly changing planet. Internal heat from deep within the planet causes continental plates to move around. Where these giant slabs collide, mountains are often pushed up. Oceans also come and go as landforms are altered. To document these changes, NASA's Earth science and space shuttle missions collect information about Earth's dynamic landscapes, oceans, and atmosphere. For example, astronauts

monitor atmospheric changes caused by air pollution and by weather conditions like El Niño.

By studying Earth's landscape, we can better understand the features on other planets. For example, by studying active shield volcanoes in Hawaii, such as Mauna Loa, scientists have a better idea how Mars's extinct shield volcanoes, like Olympus Mons, formed.

Astronauts have also traveled to and studied Earth's Moon. By collecting Moon rocks and comparing them to rocks from Earth, scientists have learned that the Moon is made up of very similar material to Earth. Some scientists hypothesize that the Moon formed from debris lofted into space when a huge object smashed into the newly forming Earth 4.5 billion years ago. Unlike Earth, the Moon has no water or air.

Shield Volcanoes

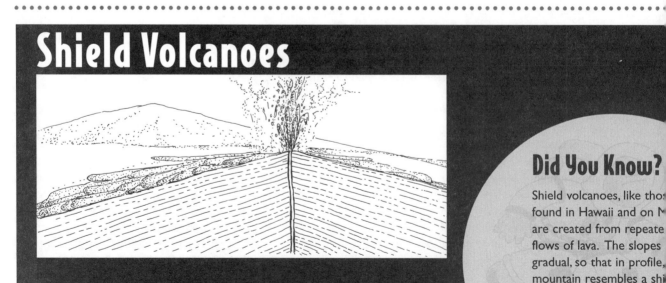

Did You Know?

Shield volcanoes, like tho: found in Hawaii and on N are created from repeate flows of lava. The slopes gradual, so that in profile, mountain resembles a shi or broad dome.

Mars

Color: red

Size: 4,222 miles across

Distance from Sun:
142 million miles

Moons: 2

Rings: none

Day (one spin):
24 hours, 37 minutes

Year (a trip around the Sun):
687 Earth days

Orbiting speed: 15 miles per second

Gravity: An 85-pound child would weigh 32 pounds.

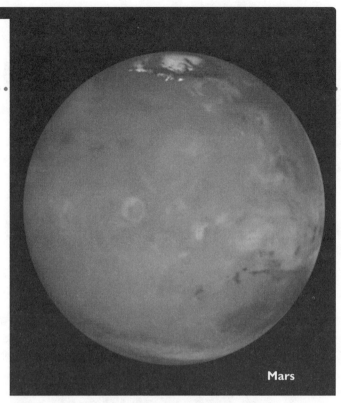

Mars

Today Mars is a cold, rock-covered desert with a thin, carbon-dioxide atmosphere. It is home to the impressive Valles Marineris canyon—which is longer than the entire United States—and the highest mountains in the solar system. Those mountains are extinct volcanoes. Mars also has polar ice caps that contain frozen water and dry ice (frozen carbon dioxide).

For several years, astronomers have been discussing whether or not life ever existed on Mars. Evidence collected from numerous space probes suggests that Mars may have once had rivers of water flowing over its surface. Liquid water is necessary to nurture even tiny organisms. Scientists have also conducted research on meteorites that fell to Earth from Mars. The research suggests to some that past Martian conditions might have supported simple life.

Scientists have been sending spacecraft to Mars for many years. In 1976, the Viking orbiters arrived at Mars and began to fly around the planet and map it and its moons, Phobos and Deimos. The Viking missions also set down robots on Mars's surface to collect photographs and scoop up soil samples for analysis. In 1996, the Mars Pathfinder and Mars Global Surveyor missions landed a rover on Mars to sample the chemistry of the rocks at different sites and to map the Martian landscape.

The best time to see Mars is about every 25 months, when Earth and Mars lie closest to each other in their orbits with a good telescope, you can even see a polar cap!

Why Are All the Rocky Planets Close to the Sun?

When the planets formed, only rocks and heavy metals, like iron, survived near the Sun's intense heat. These rocks and metals formed the small, rocky planets Mercury, Venus, Earth, and Mars. These rocky planets are also known as the "inner planets" because of their closeness to the Sun.

The rocky surface of Mars

Farther away from the Sun's heat, there were gases such as hydrogen, helium, and methane. These gases collected and formed large planets such as Jupiter and Saturn. As these planets got bigger, they attracted even more gases with their powerful gravitational fields. These large gas planets are known as the "outer planets." You will read more about them in Chapter 3.

Is Earth the Only Planet With Water?

For a long time, it was thought that water was found only on Earth. Then astronomers began finding evidence of water in many parts of the solar system.

For example, the Viking missions detected frozen water in Mars's polar ice caps. The Mars Pathfinder found evidence that suggests floods of water once flowed on Mars. Mars is not alone. Recently, the European Space Agency's Infrared Space Observatory found water in the atmospheres around some of the other planets and on Saturn's largest moon, Titan. The Lunar Prospector spacecraft has detected evidence of ice on Earth's Moon

in a deep south pole crater that is never warmed by sunlight. Photographs taken by the spacecraft Galileo of Jupiter's moon Europa show a crater that may once have been filled with water. And there is evidence that an ocean of water may exist below Europa's icy crust.

Experts believe that this water may have come from comets crashing into these planets and moons. Comets are balls of dust and ice that streak through the solar system, leaving traces of water in their path. Why is the existence of water on planets important? The presence of water on other planets means that life may be possible, or may have been possible at one time—beyond planet Earth.

Earth is known as the Blue Planet because its oceans make it appear blue from outer space.

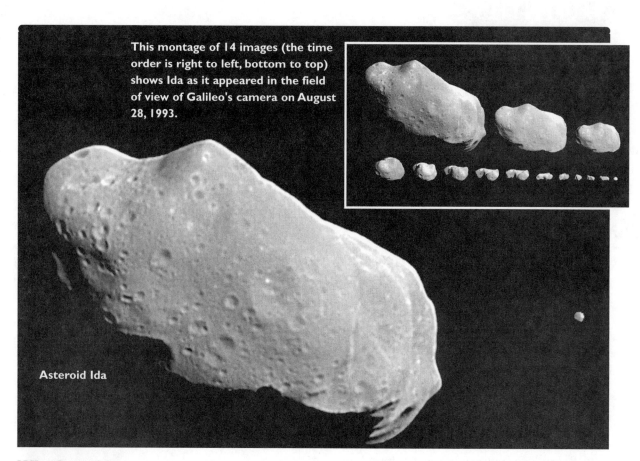

This montage of 14 images (the time order is right to left, bottom to top) shows Ida as it appeared in the field of view of Galileo's camera on August 28, 1993.

Asteroid Ida

Why Does Mars Look Red?

The soil on the surface of Mars is rich in rust (iron oxide), the same substance that forms on a steal-rimmed bicycle left out in the rain. This rust gives Mars its orange-red appearance—and its famous nickname, the Red Planet.

What Is the Asteroid Belt?

Between the orbits of Mars and Jupiter there is a large group of asteroids, or "minor planets." Some are the size of boulders; others are as big as whole states! Just like the major planets, these asteroids travel around the Sun. Although asteroids range through-out the solar system, most of them are clustered here, in the area known as the asteroid belt.

Why are there so many asteroids in one region? Some scientists believe there should have been another major planet between Mars and Jupiter. The many asteroids in this area may be pieces of a large planet that broke apart or pieces that never joined together when the other planets formed.

Did You Know?

All 5,000-plus catalogued asteroids have numbers and names.

Some are named for places:	Some are named for people:
3317 Paris	1814 Bach
2171 Kiev	1815 Beethoven
2224 Tucson	2001 Einstein
1432 Ethiopia	697 Galileo
2575 Bulgaria	1288 Santa

Readers' Theater:
The Rocky Planet Weather Report

Make copies of this Readers' Theater production (pages 39–40) and get together a cast of five students to help teach the class about planetary weather conditions. To get the whole class involved, invite some students to read the script, others to create a "set," and still others to appear in made-up television commercials before and after the weather broadcast.

Comparing Mercury and the Moon

Reproduce copies of the activity found on page 41. Invite students to observe and study photos of the surfaces of Mercury and the Moon and then encourage them to describe ways they are alike—and different.

Extension

Take your students outside to observe the Moon the next time it is visible during the day. (Check the Web site **www.moon-watch.com** for current information.) Students can observe the Moon with binoculars or a telescope during the day (but never have students look directly at the Sun with either binoculars or a telescope). Have students draw what they see on the Moon's surface. They should be able to see many craters. Some areas on the Moon also appear to be lighter, some appear to be darker. The dark spots are areas where large space rocks collided with the Moon long ago, leaving craters that were later filled in with dark basalt lava some 3 to 4 billion years ago.

Exploring the Blue Planet

Because there is a lot of water on Earth, life flourishes here. Encourage students to celebrate life on the Blue Planet by working on one or both of the following projects:

1 **Collect photographs** of water (lakes, oceans, rivers, reservoirs, even swimming pools and dripping faucets) from magazines. Use the photos to create a collage.

2 **Draw or collect pictures** of creatures that live in water or depend on water for life (just about every species!). Arrange the pictures in photo-essay form and write captions explaining why water is important to each creature.

Extension

Create a rainstorm in your classroom. Have students sit in chairs in a circle facing you. Let them know that you will be walking around in front of each of them. As you walk by, have each student imitate what you are doing until you circle around to them again. Start by making wind sounds by rubbing your hands together. Next, snap your fingers to imitate rain. Then slap your hands on your thighs to mimic a downpour. Then while slapping your hands, start stamping your feet to imitate thunder. Return to just slapping your hands, then slapping your fingers, then rubbing your hands, and then—silence. The storm has passed.

After this fun exercise, have students consult weather maps (available in most major newspapers) and almanacs to see how much rain falls on different parts of planet Earth.

Mapping Earth's Continents

Get your students thinking about where the continents are located on Earth today with this mapping challenge.

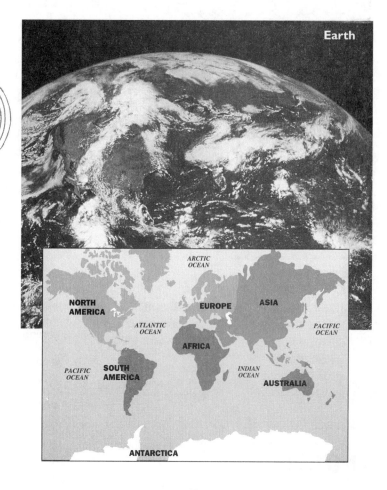

Earth

MATERIALS:

- 12 large round balloons
- a pair of scissors or a sharp knife
- 12 paper plates
- physical Earth globe
- 6 colored markers
- tape

DIRECTIONS:

1 Before class begins, blow up the balloons and knot the ends. Cut a slit in the bottom of each paper plate and stick the end of the balloon through it. Tape the end of the balloon to each paper plate to secure it. These are your model Earth globes.

2 Divide students into six small groups and give each group a model Earth globe and a marker. Have students use their markers to draw where the continents are located (from memory). Have each team share its results.

3 Introduce a real Earth globe and review the positions of the continents with your kids.

4 Give your kids some time to study this globe. Then pass out the second set of your balloon model Earth globes and have them work cooperatively again to draw the continents in their correct location.

5 Congratulate the team that showed the most improvement between its first model globe and its second.

Mars Ice Caps

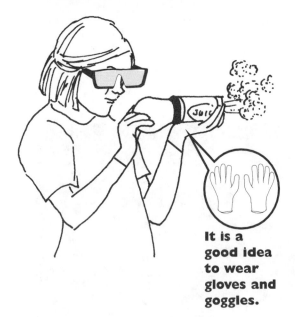

It is a good idea to wear gloves and goggles.

Mars has a thin carbon-dioxide atmosphere with polar dry ice (frozen carbon dioxide) caps. Try this experiment to introduce your students to dry ice and the process of sublimation (when molecules move directly from a solid to gas as they warm up —without appearing to become liquid in the process). Because dry ice is very cold (minus 109 degrees Fahrenheit) and can cause serious ice burns, always use tongs when handling it. It is also a good idea to wear gloves and safety goggles. DO NOT let students handle dry ice themselves.

MATERIALS:

- 1 to 2 pounds of dry ice; dry ice can be purchased at most grocery stores—ask at the checkout counter.

- small metal can with a plastic lid (a coffee can works well)
- can opener
- scissors

- balloon
- rubber band
- tongs for handling dry ice
- gloves

- hammer
- safety goggles
- large plastic bag

DIRECTIONS:

1 Cut a small hole in the middle of the plastic lid. Use a can opener to cut out the bottom of the can.

2 Next, cut the end of a balloon off and stretch it over the bottom of the can. Place a rubber band around the can to secure the edge of the balloon.

3 Put on your safety goggles first. Then place the block of dry ice in the plastic bag, and break it into smaller pieces with a hammer. Put on your gloves and pick up a small piece of ice and place it in the can. Fit the plastic lid over the top of the can.

4 Pull the bottom of the balloon away from the can and let it go with a snap. What happens? A ring of vapor will come out of the top of the can. Demonstrate this several times and ask your students what is happening. (The dry ice or carbon dioxide is colder than the air in your classroom. As the dry ice turns into gas, it cools the air around it, causing the water in the air to condense and form a small cloud.)

Mega Martian Volcanoes

The largest volcanoes in the solar system are found on Mars. The highest, Olympus Mons, is an inactive shield volcano. Shield volcanoes form from eruptions of flowing lava. With each eruption, the lava spreads out and gradually builds up wide gentle slopes—like those that formed the Hawaiian islands.

In this activity, help students compare Olympus Mons to the biggest shield volcano on Earth—Mauna Loa. Mauna Loa is 100 miles wide and 6 miles high from the ocean floor. Olympus Mons is 335 miles wide and 15 miles high. It covers a surface area bigger than the entire state of Arizona.

MATERIALS:

- copies of the reproducible found on page 42
- pencils
- scissors

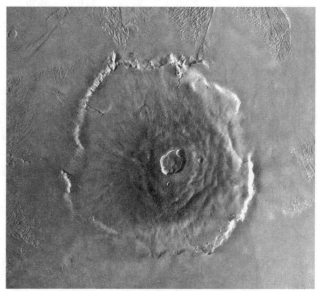
Olympus Mons

DIRECTIONS:

1 Invite students to estimate how many Mauna Loas could fit inside Olympus Mons. Record their answers on the blackboard.

2 Challenge your students to cut out the Mauna Loa model and trace as many patterns of it as they can inside Olympus Mons.

3 Ask students to share their results. (Answers should range from 7 to 9). How accurate were their estimates? Who provided the best guess?

Note: Point out to students that Olympus Mons grew so big because it was located over a Martian "hot spot" for a long time and erupted time after time. Volcanoes on Earth do not get that large because the Earth's crust is constantly moving, preventing one site from sitting atop a hot spot for very long. Instead of one volcano growing very, very large, several smaller volcanoes tend to form in a region. The Hawaiian islands are a good example of this phenomenon.

Model a Martian Landscape

Mars, like Earth, has volcanoes, mountains, canyons, valleys, rock-covered fields, and dry, sandy riverbeds. Like Earth, it also has craters that formed when meteorites struck Mars in the past. Using the pictures found on page 43, make a relief map of a Martian landscape.

MATERIALS:

- reproducible on page 43
- tag board, or large piece of heavy cardboard
- spoon
- toothpicks
- pencils
- dough (see recipe)

Dough recipe

- 6 cups salt
- 6 cups flour
- 3 cups water

Mix together the salt and flour, then add the water slowly and stir until the dough is well mixed. You will need to make several batches, depending on the number of students you have.

DIRECTIONS:

1 Invite students to study the Martian landscape images found in books and on the reproducible. What physical features (mountains, volcanoes, valleys) can they identify?

2 Divide students into small groups and distribute a pencil and a piece of tag board to each group. Encourage each group to draw a Martian landscape as it would be seen from space.

3 Next, give each student group 3 cups of dough. Challenge them to build up the volcanoes, craters and mountain ranges on their drawing and then fill in the rest of the map to the edges using the remaining dough. The dry riverbeds can be marked by making indentations with toothpicks or spoons. Small dough balls can be molded to create rocks.

4 Set the maps in a warm place to dry (this may take as long as a week). Then tape the maps together to create one giant classroom map. Invite kids to paint it using acrylic paints.

Readers' Theater: **The Rocky Planet Weather Report**

Characters:

- ● **News Anchor**
- ● **Mercury Weather Forecaster**
- ● **Venus Weather Forecaster**
- ● **Earth Weather Forecaster**
- ● **Mars Weather Forecaster**

Planet Earth

News Anchor:
Welcome to PEN—your Planetary Educational Network. I'm your host, Jordan, and it's time for another weather update from the rocky planets. Let's start by going to Mercury. Mercury, are you there?

Mercury Weather Forecaster:
Hi, Jordan! It looks like another long, hot day ahead on Mercury. We have temperatures over 800 degrees Fahrenheit and not a single cloud in sight! When night finally comes, we expect it to cool down quite a bit. In fact, temperatures will dip down to 275 degrees below zero. Now that's cold!

News Anchor:
Wow, Mercury! That's the biggest temperature drop anywhere in the solar system! I guess that's what you get when you've got no atmosphere.

Mercury Weather Forecaster:
That's right, Jordan. We don't have an atmosphere to help control our temperature. And one thing is for sure: Here on Mercury we have plenty of time to watch the weather. One day on this planet is as long as 59 days on Earth.

News Anchor:
Thanks for the report, Mercury. Let's head over to Venus now and take a look at the weather there.

Venus Weather Forecaster:
Hi, Jordan! We're looking at another cloudy day here on Venus—complete with killer smog made of sulfuric acid. Whew! Daytime temperatures are going to be around 860 degrees Fahrenheit.

CONTINUED ON NEXT PAGE

Readers' Theater: **The Rocky Planet Weather Report**

And since we have an atmosphere of carbon dioxide trapping in the heat, I don't expect the planet to cool off much tonight. We've also been seeing some lighting strikes through our orange-yellow clouds.

News Anchor:
Any signs of more lightning ahead, Venus?

Venus Weather Forecaster:
We're not seeing any right now, but we'll keep you posted. More from orange-sky country later. Meanwhile, back to you, Jordan.

News Anchor:
Thanks, Venus. Now on to Earth. What's the weather like there on our favorite Blue Planet?

Earth Weather Forecaster:
Warm sunny weather continues over much of the Earth with rain showers predicted in the southern low-lying areas. To the north, cooler weather is coming. In fact, we expect snow to fall in some of the mountains tonight. Right now, we have a lot of wet, dense fog in the valleys.

With all that moisture in the air, it can be difficult to see. But that should change as the Sun warms things up today.

News Anchor:
Any new storms brewing off the coasts?

Earth Weather Forecaster:
We're watching for some tropical storms off the coast of Florida. The wind and waves are really picking up and we may see a hurricane coming on shore soon. Back to you, Jordan.

News Anchor:
Thanks, Earth. Let's check in now with Mars.

Mars Weather Forecaster:
Greetings, Jordan! It's a comfortable 70 degrees Fahrenheit here at the Martian equator. And I don't see one cloud in the pink sky. All in all, I'd say it's a pretty nice day in this dry, desertlike area. We have had some dust storms, but it looks like we are finally getting a break. I'll tell you, though, Jordan: At the north pole here on Mars, the weather is a completely different story.

It's an icy 193 degrees below zero.

News Anchor:
And what is your long-range forecast, Mars?

Mars Weather Forecaster:
Looking ahead, we are probably in for a tough Martian winter. Last year, as you recall, temperatures dipped down to a frosty minus 220 degrees.

News Anchor:
Well, that's definitely not swimsuit weather, Mars.

Mars Weather Forecaster:
You're right, Jordan. But we would have no use for swimsuits anyway. As you know, water has not flowed around here in quite some time. The closest thing we have to a beach is the dusty red sand on our surface. We can't swim but we can dig in the sand!

News Anchor:
Thanks, Mars. Enjoy your summer while it lasts. And now we are out of time. Check this channel tonight for more weather updates and thanks for watching PEN, your Planetary Education Network.

Name_____

Comparing Mercury and the Moon

**The planet Mercury looks a lot like the Earth's Moon.
Study the pictures and do some research, then answer the questions below.**

Planet Mercury   Earth's Moon

Finish the sentence.

Mercury and the Earth's Moon look alike because.....

1. _____

2. _____

3. _____

While they look alike, Mercury and Earth's Moon are very different. Use the facts you have learned in class to underline the correct word(s) in each sentence.

1. (Mercury   Earth's Moon) orbits around the Sun.

2. (Mercury   Earth's Moon) orbits around the Earth.

3. (Mercury   Earth's Moon) has been visited by astronauts.

4. (Mercury   Earth's Moon) is too hot for astronauts to visit.

5. (Mercury   Earth's Moon) is larger than **(Mercury   Earth's Moon)**.

Name _____

Mega Martian Volcanoes

1. Estimate how many of Earth's biggest shield volcano, Mauna Loa, could fit inside Mars's biggest volcano, Olympus Mons. Write your estimate here.

_____

2. Cut out the model of Mauna Loa and trace around it as many times as you can inside Olympus Mons to check your answer. The actual number of Mauna Loas that can fit inside Olympus Mons is

_____ .

Think, Research, and Answer
Use a separate sheet of paper.

1. What is a shield volcano?

2. How did Olympus Mons get so big?

3. Can volcanoes on Earth get as big as Olympus

8°

1" wide

10" wide
Olympus Mons

8°

10°   10°

2" wide
Mauna Loa

Team Members _____

Model a Martian Landscape

Study the photographs
and do research, then
create a relief map of a
Martian landscape on tag
board. Mars, like Earth,
has mountains, canyons,
craters, volcanoes, valleys,
rock-covered fields, and
dry, sandy riverbeds.
Like Earth, Mars also has
craters that formed
when meteorites struck
the planet in the past.

**Martian
Landscape**

DIRECTIONS:

1 Study the satellite photographs
of Mars. What do you see?

_____

_____

_____

_____

_____

2 On a piece of tag board or
cardboard, draw a map of
a Martian landscape as if you
were looking at it from space.
Outline physical features like
volcanoes, mountains, valleys,
canyons and dry riverbeds.

3 Now get some salt dough
from your teacher. Use the
dough to shape the volcanoes,
craters, and mountain ranges in
3-D (three dimensions). Place
these dough features on your map.

4 Fill in the rest of the map to
the edges by spreading the
remaining dough in a flat layer. Use
toothpicks or a spoon to mark dry
riverbeds. Mold some small dough
balls to look like rocks. Add them
to your map.

5 When you are finished, let
your map dry for one week.
Share your map with others.

Background Information

The Gas Planets

Jupiter, Saturn, Uranus, and Neptune are all commonly called the "gas planets." Located far away from the Sun, they are immense, rapidly spinning bodies of gas. The gas planets have no solid surface. They also have very low density, or weight for their size. For example, Saturn's density is so low that if you had a large enough bath tub, the planet would actually float! All giant gas planets have large and complex storm systems and clouds. They also have rings of rock, ice, and space dust that encircle them.

Pluto is not a giant gas planet, but lies beyond them. Pluto is unique among the planets in our solar system. It is much smaller than the other planets and is made of a mixture of ice and rock.

Jupiter

Color: brown and beige striped

Size: 88,849 miles across

Distance from Sun: 484 million miles

Moons: 16

Rings: yes

Day (one spin): 9 hours, 52 minutes

(the fastest spinner of all the planets!)

Year (a trip around the Sun): 11.9 Earth years

Orbiting speed: 8 miles per second

Gravity: An 85-pound child would weigh 216 pounds.

Jupiter, our largest planet, is a swirling ball of mostly hydrogen gas. It has no solid surface, but scientists think that far below Jupiter's surface is a small, rocky core. Intense pressure within Jupiter's interior causes its hydrogen gas to exist in a metallic liquid form. Above this are colorful bands of clouds that circle the planet. These swirling clouds give the planet its striped appearance. Jupiter is also known for its Great Red Spot, an immense hurricanelike storm.

No space probe will ever land on Jupiter because there is no solid surface. However, spacecraft have circled and photographed this giant planet. In 1979, the Voyager 1 & 2 spacecraft took pictures of Jupiter and its moons. The pictures revealed that Jupiter had thin rings of dust and ice. In 1995, the Galileo spacecraft sent a probe into Jupiter which collected atmospheric information. The Galileo spacecraft continues to circle Jupiter and send back pictures of its moons. The Galileo mission has revealed some interesting news: Jupiter's rings are still expanding! As asteroids collide with Jupiter, they splatter more dust and ice into orbit around the planet.

Jupiter can be seen for about ten months of the year.

This photo collage shows Jupiter (bottom left) and four of its moons. The moons are, from left: Io, Europa, Ganymede, and Callisto.

Saturn

Color: yellow and brown

Size: 74,899 miles across

Distance from the Sun: 888 million miles

Moons: at least 18

Rings: yes

Day (one spin): 10 hours, 40 minutes

Year (a trip around the Sun): 29.5 Earth years

Orbiting speed: 6 miles per second

Gravity: An 85-pound child would weigh 92 pounds.

Like the other giant gas planets, Saturn has no solid surface. Instead it has a hot churning core surrounded by a layer of liquid-hydrogen. It also has an atmosphere with thin clouds of water and ammonia. Storm spots and super strong icy winds blow constantly in Saturn's atmosphere. Orbiting around the planet are billions of small pieces of ice, dust, and rock. These particles—some as small as specks and others as large as skyscrapers—form Saturn's famous rings.

Voyager spacecraft's 1 and 2 flew past at Saturn in 1980 and 1981. They showed that Saturn's six major rings were organized into thousands of "ringlets." These missions also uncovered a great deal of information about Saturn's moons. For example, the missions showed that two of Saturn's moons, Pandora and Prometheus, keep the particles in one of Saturn's rings together by tugging on the particles with their gravitational pulls. The Voyager missions also discovered that Saturn's largest moon, Titan, has a nitrogen-based atmosphere, similar to Earth's atmosphere shortly after it formed.

Experts say more news about Saturn should be on the way soon. The Cassini spacecraft, launched in 1997, will reach Saturn in 2004. Cassini will study Saturn's atmosphere and magnetic field. It will also drop a probe into the atmosphere of Titan in the hope of learning more about Saturn's biggest moon.

Saturn is the farthest planet that can be seen without a telescope. Because it only moves through one zodiac constellation every two and a half years, it is easy to find in the sky. It can be seen sometime during the night through most of the year.

Uranus

Color: green

Size: 31,764 miles across

Distance from Sun: 1,783 million miles

Moons: 18

Rings: yes

Day (one spin): 17 hours, 14 minutes

Year (a trip around the Sun): 84 Earth years

Orbiting speed: 4 miles per second

Gravity: An 85-pound child would weigh 76 pounds.

Uranus is a spinning ball of gas about four times wider than Earth. It has a rocky core covered by layers of very hot water, ammonia, and methane (natural gas). Above these hot churning gases, clouds of frozen methane swirl around in a chilly atmosphere of hydrogen and helium gas. Uranus rotates on its side. It may have been knocked over at some point when an asteroid or other space object crashed into it.

Much of what we know about Uranus came from the Voyager 2 mission in 1986. The Voyager 2 took photographs of Uranus and confirmed what astronomers had long suspected—that Uranus has a faint set of rings. Uranus's rings are made up of black, boulder-size rocks. These rocks may be pieces of moons that broke apart long ago. Voyager 2 also discovered that Uranus had 15 moons, not merely 5 as scientists had previously believed. One of these moons, Miranda, appears to have been broken apart at one point and then recollected. Its surface contains many large craters and cracks.

Uranus cannot be seen without the aid of a telescope.

Did You Know?

Many of Uranus's moons are named after characters in Shakespeare's plays. For example, the moon "Puck" is named after a character from *A Midsummer Night's Dream*.

The Gas Planets — Jupiter, Saturn, Uranus and Neptune.

Neptune

Color: greenish blue

Size: 30,776 miles across

Distance from Sun: 2,797 million miles

Moons: 8

Rings: yes

Day (one spin): 16 hours, 7 minutes

Year (a trip around the Sun): 164.8 Earth years

Orbiting speed: 3.2 miles per second

Gravity: An 85-pound child would weigh 98 pounds.

Neptune is a spinning ocean of hot gases. There is no solid ground. Instead, a thick atmosphere of hydrogen, helium, and methane stretches over a liquid surface. Winds can reach speeds of 1,000 miles per hour! The blue color of Neptune comes from the high levels of methane in its thick gaseous atmosphere. Neptune also once had a large storm system called the Great Dark Spot that rotates around the planet counterclockwise. This storm was a lot like a cyclone, or tornado, on Earth. The storm has disappeared since the Voyager space craft flew by in 1989. Experts believe Neptune's storms may come and go.

Voyager 2, which flew by Neptune in 1989 after a 12-year journey, is the only space probe to have visited the planet so far. This mission showed that Neptune had five distinct rings and a total of eight moons. Voyager also discovered some facts about Neptune's largest moon, Triton. Images from the spacecraft show that Triton has geysers that spew nitrogen gas and dust into its thin atmosphere.

Neptune can only be seen with a telescope.

Pluto

Color: gray

Size: 1,420 miles across

Distance from Sun: 3,596 million miles

Moons: 1

Rings: none

Day (one spin): 6 Earth days, 9 hours

Year (a trip around the Sun): 248 Earth years

Orbiting speed: 3 miles per second

Gravity: An 85-pound child would weigh 5 pounds.

The farthest planet from the Sun, Pluto is also the most mysterious planet in our solar system. As mentioned at the start of this chapter, Pluto is neither a rocky planet nor a giant gas planet. Pluto is composed instead of a mixture of rock and ice. It has a low density like the giant gas planets, but unlike them, Pluto is very small.

Because Pluto is so different from the other planets in our solar system, many scientists question whether Pluto should really be classified as a planet at all. Some scientists think Pluto was once a moon of Neptune that fell out of orbit. Others think Pluto is merely an asteroid or stray icy body that was not absorbed by the gas planets when they formed long ago.

Like Uranus, Pluto spins on its side. Its surface is covered in methane ice. The planet's thin atmosphere of gases thaws when Pluto is closer to the Sun and freezes again as it moves away. Pluto has one moon, Charon, that is close in size to Pluto and covered in frozen water. Some astronomers think Pluto and Charon should be recognized as a double planet.

Pluto can only been seen through large, powerful telescopes. The best images of Pluto to date have come from the U.S. space agency's Hubble Space Telescope. Pluto has the distinction of being the only planet that has not been studied by a spacecraft from Earth.

Frequently Asked Questions

Why Do the Gas Planets Have Rings?

Jupiter, Saturn, Uranus, and Neptune all have rings of dust and ice circling them. Recently, NASA's Galileo spacecraft helped scientists understand how those rings formed. Pictures taken by the spacecraft showed that meteoroids were striking Jupiter's inner moons and kicking up particles of dust. The moons—Metis, Adrastea, Amalthea, and Thebe—have very little gravity to pull the dust toward their surfaces. Therefore, the dust flies off into space and begins to circle Jupiter, which has high gravity. Astronomers believe that ring systems around the other gas planets probably formed in a similar way. Because the rocky planets generally have fewer moons and less gravity, rings are less likely to form around these planets.

Saturn

Is Pluto Always the Farthest Planet From the Sun?

No. Pluto is usually the most distant planet in our solar system, but not always. For a short period every 232 years or so, Neptune takes that honor. The reason is that Pluto has an unusually shaped orbit that brings it within Neptune's path. When Pluto crosses inside Neptune's orbit, Pluto lies closer to the Sun, and Neptune becomes the farthest planet. This phenomenon occurred from 1979 to 1999. It will happen again starting in 2231.

When Will a Spacecraft Land on the Gas Planets?

Never. It would be impossible to land a spacecraft on the giant gas planets because none of them have a solid surface. In addition, the tremendous heat and pressure below the clouds would destroy any spacecraft that tried to get too close. However, scientists have learned amazing things about the gas planets even without landing a spacecraft. For example, the spacecraft Galileo was launched in 1989 to explore Jupiter and its moons. It did not land on Jupiter, but circled the planet and took thousands of photographs. These images have taught astronomers a great deal about Jupiter and its moons.

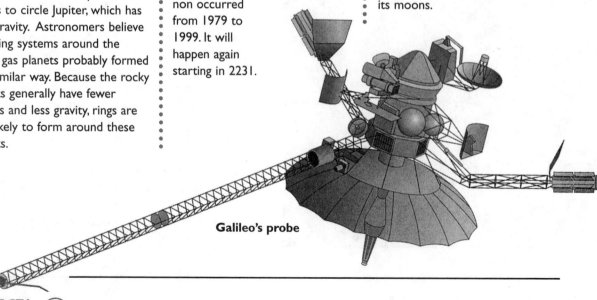
Galileo's probe

Readers' Theater:
The Gas Planet Weather Report

Copy five sets of this Readers' Theater production (pages 52–53) and get together a cast of students to help teach the whole class about planetary weather conditions.

Puzzling Pluto

Pluto is an odd planet. It is not a giant gas planet; instead, it is the smallest planet in our solar system. Astronomers have different theories about how it was formed. Use the reproducible on page 58 to examine some of these ideas, and see what your students think.

Great Planetary Graph

Using the reproducible found on page 59, help your students graph the distance between the planets.

Design Your Own Minor Planet

Enhance your study of planets by sharing a delightful classic with your children, *The Little Prince* by Antoine de Saint-Exupery (Harcourt Brace Jovanovich, 1961). In this fictional story, a little prince lives on a tiny planet (or "asteroid"). When he leaves it to explore other planets, he makes new discoveries about life and death. After you have read part of this story to your students, have them design their own imaginary planet.

Picture Jupiter

Most images of planets are *composites* (where a larger picture is created by putting together many smaller pictures). Smaller pictures, taken by satellites or the Hubble Space Telescope, can be reassembled by a computer to produce a larger image. Help your students create a composite picture of Jupiter's surface by cutting apart the smaller pictures and putting them together in the correct order.

MATERIALS:

- scissors
- reproducible found on page 51
- tape
- crayons

DIRECTIONS:

1 Show students some images of Jupiter. Explain to them that scientists use computers to put together smaller pictures of a planet to create larger images. (Have them look carefully at photographs of planets that you may have in the classroom. Can they see any tiny lines in the image where the smaller pictures come together?)

2 Distribute the reproducible and help students tape together their larger picture of Jupiter. Encourage them to color the individual cloud bands and storm spots in contrasting colors. (By choosing different sets of colors, the detail in the banded structure and the spots can be enhanced).

3 When students are finished coloring their images of Jupiter, pin their pictures on a bulletin board and have students pick which image has the best enhancement. Remind them that most color pictures of planets are enhanced this way using computers so a planet's features stand out.

MINI-BOOK
Saturn's Ears

Saturn's Ears is a mini-book for your kids to make and read. Make photocopies of page 54 and distribute one to each student. Have them fold the book along the dotted lines as shown.

While working on the mini-books, share some background about Galileo Galilei with your students. Galileo was a clever Renaissance scientist. In 1609 he built a new telescope and looked up to the sky. He discovered that Earth's Moon had mountains and that Jupiter had moons of its own. He also discovered "ears" (rings) for Saturn. One of Galileo's most significant discoveries was that Venus moved around the Sun. Armed with this understanding, Galileo theorized that Earth orbited around the Sun too—just as the scientist Copernicus had proposed in the early 1500s. This theory upset Catholic Church officials who supported the idea that the Earth was the center of the universe. The church's Inquisition found Galileo guilty of heresy in 1633 and Galileo spent the rest of his life under house arrest. Even then, he continued to explore the sky.

Calculate Your Weight on Earth, Jupiter, and Pluto

The force of gravity determines what a person weighs. On some planets, like Jupiter, the gravitational pull is strong, so people would weigh more there than they do on Earth. On other planets, like Pluto, the gravitational pull is weak, so people would weigh less. Distribute copies of the reproducible found on page 57 and help kids determine what they would weigh on Earth, Jupiter, and Pluto.

Comparing Gases

Uranus and Neptune are made up of methane, hydrogen, helium, ammonia, and water vapor. These gases are also abundant on Earth and we use them every day. Distribute the reproducible found on page 56 and invite your kids to unscramble the common use of each gas.

Neptune's Spinning Rings

The rings around Neptune (or any of the gas planets) are not solid. Neptune's rings are actually particles of rocks, dust, and ice that are constantly spinning around the planet. Their movement makes them appear to be solid rings. To help your students understand this concept, help them assemble a pattern of Neptune's rings.

MATERIALS:

● reproducible found on page 55

● pencils

● pins or tacks

DIRECTIONS:

1 Distribute a copy of page 55 to each child. Have children cut out the rings pattern and attach it to a pencil eraser with a pin.

2 Invite students to hypothesize what will happen when they spin the pattern. Record their responses and let them give the pattern a spin. What do they see? (When spinning, the rocks form rings.) How many different rings do they see? (Neptune has two outer rings and two lighter inner rings.)

Name _____

Picture Jupiter

Cut apart the small pictures and put them in the correct order to create a larger image of Jupiter. Then color the individual cloud bands and storm spots in contrasting colors.

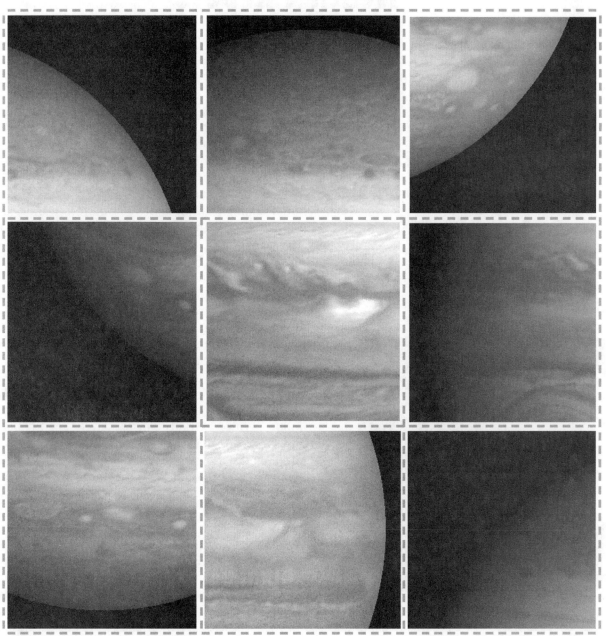

Readers' Theater: **The Gas Planet Weather Report**

Characters:

- **News Anchor**
- **Jupiter Weather Forecaster**
- **Saturn Weather Forecaster**
- **Uranus Weather Forecaster**
- **Neptune Weather Forecaster**
- **Pluto Weather Forecaster**

Saturn

News Anchor:
Welcome to PEN — your Planetary Educational Network. I'm your host, Jordan, and it's time for a weather update from the gas planets. Let's get started today talking with Jupiter. Jupiter, are you there?

Jupiter Weather Forecaster:
Hi, Jordan! It's looking like another stormy day here on Jupiter. Winds are picking up to the west and our 350-year-old hurricane, the Great Red Spot, just keeps gaining energy. It is stirring up this ocean of gas, and more storms are expected to follow. With icy clouds moving overhead, all in all, it is just a typical day on the big planet. Back to you, Jordan.

News Anchor:
Anything exciting happening on any of your moons today, Jupiter?

Jupiter Weather Forecaster:
We're expecting to see some more volcanoes erupting today on Io, Jordan. We've got a plume of gas rising over there and we'll be watching it.

News Anchor:
Thanks, Jupiter. Let's get a Saturn update next. Saturn, are you there?

Saturn Weather Forecaster:
Yikes, it's cold here, Jordan. We've got 1,000-mile-an-hour winds blowing right now with a few storms moving overhead. If you consider that hurricane winds on Earth begin at 45 miles an hour, you can see how nothing could stand upright on Saturn. Actually, there's nothing to stand on anyway in this frosty ocean of hydrogen!

News Anchor:
Saturn, what's happening out on your rings?

Saturn Weather Forecaster:
Jordan, we're expecting the rings to get a little bigger as more space garbage passes nearby. By garbage, I mean rocks, ice, and dust.

News Anchor:
Thanks for the update, Saturn. We've got to check in with Uranus now. Uranus, are you there?

Uranus Weather Forecaster:
Hi, Jordan. We're looking at another icy day here today. Temperature in the upper atmosphere is minus 350 degrees Fahrenheit with green clouds moving in this afternoon. For all you Sun lovers though, there's good news. You can expect sunshine on the north pole for the next 40 years. For all you night owls on the south pole, you know the story—it's dark, real dark.

News Anchor:
Uranus, any updates from your moon Miranda today?

Uranus Weather Forecaster:
On Miranda, we are expecting to see dry, cold weather. No new news to report on last week's meteorite strike, but Miranda has seen a lot worse. Remember when Miranda got hit so hard it busted apart and had to recollect itself?

News Anchor:
I sure do. That's a mighty tough moon there. Thanks, Uranus. Let's catch up with Neptune now. Neptune, are you there?

Neptune Weather Forecaster:
Greetings from big blue, Jordan. It's a beautiful day to sail across this giant hot tub of water and gas. Winds are picking up a little to the south, and we expect to see some stronger storms and a few clouds, but all in all it's a great day!

News Anchor:
Neptune, what can we expect for the weekend?

Neptune Weather Forecaster:
More of the same. It'll be cold, so bundle up!

News Anchor:
Thanks, Neptune. Let's wrap up here today by checking in with our unusual friend, Pluto. Pluto, are you there?

Pluto Weather Forecaster:
I'm here, Jordan. We've got a little cold haze here today, but as we move farther away from the Sun, all that will freeze. It is probably going to be as slick as a skating rink soon.

News Anchor:
Pluto, is there any sunshine ahead in your forecast?

Pluto Weather Forecaster:
Out here, Jordan, the Sun just looks like a bright star in the sky. There's not much sunlight ahead. Just more cold and dark conditions.

News Anchor:
Thanks, Pluto. That's all the time we have today. Thanks again for tuning in to PEN, your Planetary Educational Network. See you tomorrow.

Mini-Book: Saturn's Ears

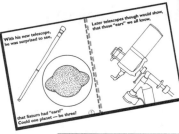

Color the pictures and cut along the solid line.
Fold along the dotted lines to make your mini-book.

③

In later years, telescopes would show
that those "ears" we all know . . .

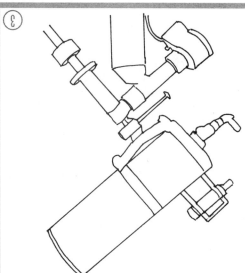

②

that Saturn had "ears"!
Could one planet — be three?

With his new telescope,
he was surprised to see

were really ice and dust, in fact,
circling around Saturn in a wide track.

④

In the year 1610,
Galileo looked at Saturn again.

①

Name _____

Neptune's Spinning Rings

Cut the pattern out around the dotted edge. Push a pin through the center of the pattern and then into the eraser of a pencil. Give the pattern a spin. What do you see?

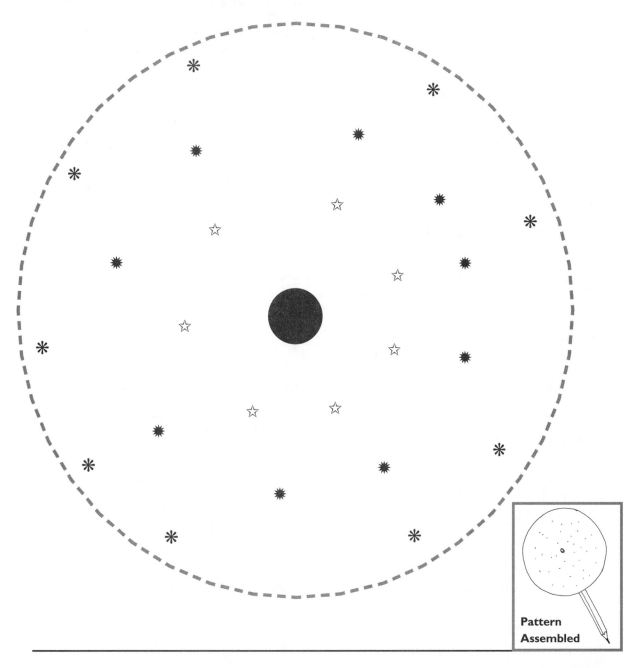

Pattern Assembled

Name _____

Comparing Gases

Uranus and Neptune are made up of hydrogen, helium, methane, ammonia, and water vapor. These gases are also found on Earth. Read each clue below. Then unscramble the words to figure out how we use some of these gases every day.

1. Methane, or natural gas, is found in the clouds that surround Uranus. Methane is also the gas we burn in a __ __ __ __ __ __ __ __ to keep a house warm.
Unscramble: CAUFREN

2. Helium swirls around Neptune. It is a very light gas. On Earth, helium is put in __ __ __ __ __ __ __ __ and __ __ __ __ __ __ so they can float in the air.
Unscramble: LONSABLO   SMLBPI

3. Water vapor is water in its gaseous form. It appears in the atmospheres of many planets. On Earth, we find water vapor naturally in __ __ __ __ __ __ __ and __ __ __ __ . We also use it in some appliances, like irons.
Unscramble: SOUCDL   OGF

4. A common gas on Uranus is ammonia. On Earth, we use ammonia in many products, including __ __ __ __ __ __ __ __ __ __ __, which we put on plants to help them grow.
Unscramble: FRIZERTIEL

5. Hydrogen is the lightest gas known to exist. The gas planets have a lot of hydrogen in their atmospheres. On Earth, hydrogen is found in __ __ __ __ __ __ __ __ __ __. These devices, which we use to power radios
Unscramble: STBERTAIE
and cars, give off small amounts of hydrogen every time they are charged.

Name _____

Calculate Your Weight

Gravity can really get you down! After all, gravity is the force that pulls you to Earth. The force of gravity also determines what you weigh. On some planets, like Jupiter, the gravitational pull is so strong that you would weigh more than you do on Earth. On other planets, like Pluto, the gravitational pull is weaker, so you would weigh less.

Try calculating what you would weigh on these planets.

1. First, step on a scale and calculate how much you weigh on Earth.

I weigh _____ pounds on Earth.

2. Next, calculate what you would weigh on Jupiter. An object on Jupiter would weigh 250 percent (2.5 times) what it weighs on Earth.

Example:

One pop can on Earth   2.5 pop cans on Jupiter

Multiply your Earth weight: _____ x 2.5 = _____ pounds (your weight on Jupiter)!

3. Now calculate what you would weigh on Pluto. An object on Pluto only weighs 6 percent (.06) of what it does on Earth.

Example:

One pop can on Earth   .06 pop cans on Pluto

Multiply your Earth weight:_____ x .06 = _____ pounds (your weight on Pluto)!

Circle the correct answer.

4. On which planet would you weigh the most? (**Earth / Jupiter / Pluto**)

5. On which planet would you weigh the least? (**Earth / Jupiter / Pluto**)

Name _____

Puzzling Pluto

Pluto is the smallest planet in our solar system. Unlike the rocky or giant gas planets, Pluto is made up mostly of ice, frozen methane gas, and rock. Astronomers are not sure how Pluto formed. Some astronomers also question whether Pluto should really be listed as a planet.

DIRECTIONS:

Read two scientists' ideas below and then write your theory about Pluto on a separate sheet of paper.

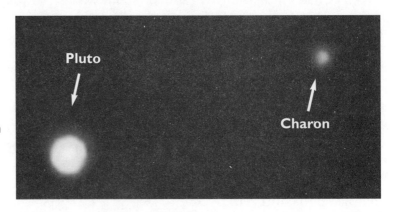

Dr. Angela's theory

Pluto may have been one of Neptune's moons. At some point, another space object crashed into Pluto. Pluto spun away from Neptune and started to orbit the Sun on its own. Pluto is now a planet. It has an atmosphere and it has a moon. Pluto also orbits around the Sun on its own predictable path. Since Pluto was first discovered in 1930, it has been recognized by the International Astronomical Society as the ninth planet in our solar system. There is no reason to change that.

Dr. Bob's theory

Pluto should not be recognized by the International Astronomical Society as a major planet. Pluto is really just a jumble of rock and ice that did not get absorbed by the gas planets when they formed. Pluto is instead a large asteroid orbiting around the Sun like so many others. There are many of small icy objects located at about the same distance from the Sun as Pluto. Pluto and Charon are just the largest of these distant icy bodies.

Think and Answer

1. How do you think Pluto formed?
2. Should Pluto be listed as a planet, or is it just an asteroid? Explain your opinion.
3. What scientific evidence supports your idea? Give at least one piece of evidence.

Example:

I agree with Dr. Angela that Pluto probably began as a moon of Neptune. But today, it is a planet. After all, it has an atmosphere and circles the Sun, just like the other planets do. Pluto should still be called a planet. To take Pluto off the planet list would just confuse people.

Name _____

Great Planetary Graph

Using the information from the box below, graph the distance between the planets.

Place an X where each planet belongs on the graph and label it.

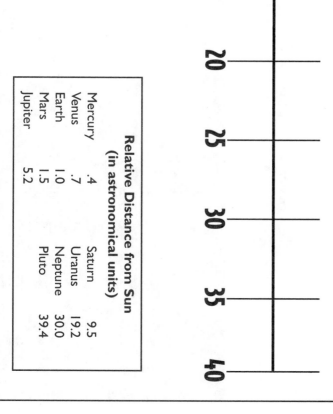

SUN

0 5 10 15 20 25 30 35 40

Relative Distance from Sun (in astronomical units)			
Mercury	.4	Saturn	9.5
Venus	.7	Uranus	19.2
Earth	1.0	Neptune	30.0
Mars	1.5	Pluto	39.4
Jupiter	5.2		

Background Information

Studying the Planets

For more than 40 years, the U.S. National Aeronautics and Space Administration (NASA) has launched spacecraft into the solar system to study the planets. Using flyby spacecraft, orbiters, atmospheric probes, and landers, NASA has closely studied all of the planets except Pluto. Pluto has only been observed using the Hubble Space Telescope.

Spacecraft Basics

Orbiters: circle around a planet

Probes: drop into a planet's atmosphere.

Landers: set down onto a planet's surface.

Rovers: move over the surface of a planet.

Space Telescopes: orbit Earth beyond its atmosphere and take pictures.

Future Planned Planeta[r]

Name	Purpose
Europa Orbiter	Spacecraft to orbit Jupit[er] moon, Europa, and mea[sure] liquid water underneath [its] icy surface.
Pluto-Keiper Express	Flyby study of Pluto and moon, Charon.
Mercury Polar Flyby	Orbiter to take pictures [of] Mercury's polar regions [and] hemisphere.

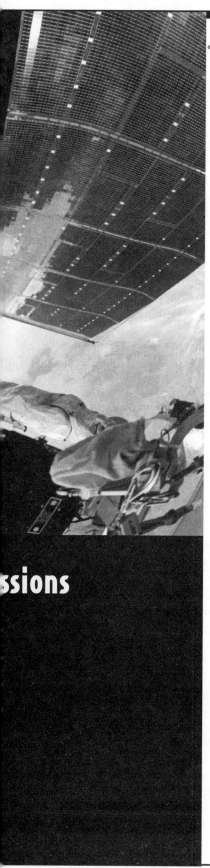

ssions

Key Planetary Visits by U.S. Spacecraft

Launch Date	Spacecraft	Purpose/Achievements
1962	Mariner 2	First successful flyby of Venus.
1969	Apollo 11	First piloted landing on Earth's Moon.
1972	Pioneer 10	Flew by Jupiter (1976) and took photos. Left the solar system (1983).
1975	Viking 1 & 2	Two spacecraft arrived at Mars (1976). Part of each spacecraft orbited around the planet, the other part landed on the surface.
1977	Voyager 1	Flew by Jupiter (1979) and Saturn (1980).
1977	Voyager 2	Flew by Jupiter (1979), Saturn (1981), Uranus (1986), and Neptune (1989) and took photos before leaving the solar system.
1989	Magellan	This orbiter made radar maps of Venus.
1989	Galileo	Is now Orbiting Jupiter (started in 1995).
1990	Hubble Telescope	The first orbiting telescope to be launched; it provides better images of the planets than ground-based telescopes looking through Earth's atmosphere.
1996	Mars Pathfinder	This lander bounced onto Mars (1997) and sent back photos and chemical analyses of rocks with the help of its Sojourner rover.
1996	Mars Global Surveyor	Orbiter to study surface features, atmosphere, and magnetic properties.
1997	Cassini	This study of Saturn and its moon, Titan, will begin in 2004.
1998	International Space Station	The first modules of this space lab were launched and joined together in 1998. Once completed, this laboratory will orbit the Earth and allow scientists to study our planet from space.
1998	Lunar Prospector	Orbiter to collect data on the Moon's poles, surface chemistry, and magnetic and gravitational fields.
1999	Mars Polar Lander	This spacecraft was supposed to land on Mars and collect information about its polar regions. The craft never landed.
1999	Mars Climate	This spacecraft was supposed to orbit Mars and collect Orbiter information about its atmosphere. The mission failed.

How Do We Get Spacecraft to Other Planets?

Most spacecraft, like Gemini, Cassini, or the space shuttle, are launched into space using rockets. Rockets push away from Earth's gravitational pull using the explosive force from burning hydrogen gas. Rockets carry satellites, space telescopes, orbiters, and probes into outer space.

What Happens to a Spacecraft When Its Mission Is Done?

It depends on the type of craft. The space shuttle is unique because it is a reusable spacecraft. After being rocketed into space with astronauts and cargo aboard, it can be piloted like a glider and returned safely to Earth. Other spacecraft never return to Earth. Most of them orbit until they run out of power or are destroyed in the harsh environment of space. Some landers, like Mars Pathfinder's Sojourner rover, remain on the planet they were sent to. Probes, like the Galileo probe, are often intentionally destroyed in the process of doing experiments.

Flyby spacecraft, like Pioneer 10 and Voyager 1 and 2, actually leave our solar system when they are finished with their missions. The Voyager spacecraft are now more than 5 billion miles away from Earth, but they are still sending back some information. On board the Voyager spacecraft are records of sounds and scenes from Earth, intended for any intelligent life that might encounter the craft.

Voyager 2

How Do Spacecraft Send Information Back to Earth?

Orbiters and probes send information back to Earth electronically, like a cellular phone or fax machine does. Radio signals send information from a transmitting antenna on a spacecraft to a receiving antenna on Earth. This information is then put into a computer for scientists to process and study.

Will Humans Ever Travel to Another Planet?

While six different missions have landed astronauts on Earth's Moon, no human has ever been to another planet. NASA hopes to send astronauts to Mars in the future. A manned mission to Mars would take more than seven years from its launch date to its return. Before taking on such a huge venture, NASA scientists are considering several important questions, including:

- Should humans go on such a mission? What can we gain?
- Is there broad public support for such a project?

- Can the United States afford such an expensive project?
- Are we technologically capable of sending people to Mars?

In the meantime, the International Space Station that is currently being assembled in space will allow astronauts from the United States, Canada, European nations, Russia, and Japan to live and work in space for extended periods of time. Scientists hope to learn how long-term stays in space affect these astronauts; this information will give us a better idea of how to prepare astronauts for future inter-planetary travel.

Are There More Planets in Other Solar Systems?

Although only nine planets orbit our Sun, other planets have been detected orbiting other stars. For example, a giant gas planet twice the size of Jupiter is orbiting a star called 47 Ursae Majoris—200 trillion miles away from Earth. To date, scientists have identified more than 30 other potential giant gas planets and have even watched a new planet.

Astronaut in space

Are There Other Earth-like Worlds?

In recent years, scientists have discovered planets in other solar systems. All of the new planets discovered to date are large gas planets. But experts believe that within these newly discovered solar systems, there could be smaller rocky planets (like Earth). Better space telescopes in the future may help us locate and photograph smaller Earth-like planets, some of which may even be capable of supporting life. For example, in 2010, NASA plans to launch the Planet Finder, a series of telescopes that would orbit Jupiter. These telescopes would work together to identify distant Earth-size planets orbiting around their own stars.

Has Life Been Found on Other Planets?

In August of 1996, a team of scientists announced that organic material (material containing the ingredients needed for life) had been found in a Martian meteorite. Some scientists think this material may be evidence of ancient Martian living things. Other scientists, however, believe the evidence is inconclusive. Research is continuing on this exciting find.

Play:
We Are the Planets

In this exciting play (page 68), several earthlings go on a tour of the solar system. Distribute copies of the play to your students, and have actors read the parts aloud. After a few practice runs, don costumes and props and perform for an audience.

Poem:
Star Gazers

By now, your students are probably looking for planets every chance they get. To encourage their interest, share the following poem either by reading it aloud or copying it onto a piece of chart paper to recite chorally.

Look up dear friend,
What do you see?
I see autos and streetlights
And smog without end.

Higher dear friend,
Now do you see?
I see buildings and airplanes
And clouds now and then.

Up and out and
Beyond all of this
Is sky and space
You won't want to miss.

Now I see, I see,
I behold it all.
Was I blind all these years?
Did I miss my call?

I see the Sun as it sets
While twilight's curtain descends.
I see planets and clusters
And galaxies without end.

Meteors! And moonbeams!
More stars than the streetlights.
It all twinkles and gleams.
What a wonderful sight.

I'm now a Star Gazer,
It's the source of my bliss.
Cause I looked up and out
And beyond all of this.

(From "Merlin's Tour of the Universe" by Neil de Grasse Tyson, Doubleday Publishing Company, 1997. Reprinted with permission.)

Rockets Away

Assemble rockets with your students and have a great time launching them! Your students will discover how rockets make it possible for us to explore other planets.

MATERIALS:

- copies of pages 72–73 for each student (Photocopy the rocket pattern on heavy stock paper: 60–100 index stock.)

- plastic 35mm film canisters with internal-sealing lid (you'll need one per child—these are usually available free of charge at camera stores)

- tape
- scissors
- Alka-Seltzer tablets
- cup of water
- paper towels
- eye protection
- tape measure

DIRECTIONS:

1 Invite some parents into your classroom to help your students assemble their rockets. Prior to the activity, put together a couple of rockets so your volunteer parents can see the finished product.

2 Pass out the rocket assembly directions, a rocket pattern, scissors, tape, and an empty film canister. Have children cut out the rocket pattern pieces and tape them to the film canister as shown on the student directions.

3 Once students have their rockets assembled (this will take about an hour), have them line the rockets up against a wall. Tape a tape measure onto the wall from the floor up.

4 Have everyone put on their eye protection, and, one at a time, give each student a half tablet of Alka-Seltzer and a little water to put into the film canister.

5 Working quickly, help each student turn the rocket upside down, fill the canister one third full with water, drop a tablet in, and snap on the lid. Place the rocket upright on the floor and stand back.

6 See whose rocket will go the highest. Try adding more water and a whole tablet to some rockets. What happens? Try adding hot water and cold water; is there any change?

Extension

Discuss the geometric shapes in a rocket (i.e., circles, cones, cylinders, triangles, rectangles). Let students design their own rocket patterns to see if the shape of the rocket changes its flight. Invite your kids to write about where they would like to send their rockets to help reinforce their understanding of planets.

Design a Planet Rover

On July 4, 1997, the Mars Pathfinder spacecraft bounced onto Mars. Surrounded by air bags, the lander came to a stop, unfolded its petals, and set the Sojourner rover onto the surface of Mars. The Sojourner rover then began to analyze and take pictures of Martian rocks and soil. Spark your students' interest in this extraordinary rover by helping them design and test their own rover. Rover tests can be conducted on a classroom floor or on the Martian landscape you created earlier in your planet unit (see page 38).

MATERIALS:

(Any combination of these will work.)

- balloons
- rubber bands
- paper plates
- straws
- skewers
- toilet paper rolls
- pipe cleaners
- washers
- tape
- scissors
- small boxes
- dowels cut up into 1" to 6" pieces

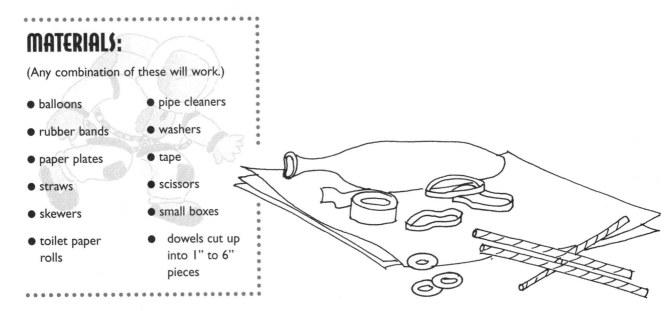

DIRECTIONS:

1 Blow up a balloon and let it go. Which way does it move? (The balloon moves in the opposite direction of the air that is being released from inside.) Why? (Newton's Third Law of Motion: For every action, there is an equal and opposite reaction.) Remind students that rockets work on this same principle.

2 Set out an assortment of supplies and challenge students to design their own balloon-powered rovers. The only design criteria are that each rover should have a balloon

attached to it—and that the rover should move as air is released from the balloon. Encourage your kids to experiment!

3 Give students about an hour to put together their first rover. Then have students blow up their balloons, set the rovers on the classroom floor, and release their balloons. Which rover traveled the farthest? (Can any of your rovers move over your Martian landscape?)

Did You Know?

The Sojourner rover was named by Valerie Ambroise, a 12-year-old girl from Connecticut. Valerie won the rover-naming contest with an essay on Sojourner Truth, an African-American woman who fought against slavery and championed women's rights during the Civil War era.

Mission to Mars

NASA is planning a manned mission to Mars. The trip will take more than seven years. Travel time between Earth and Mars will take more than $2\frac{1}{2}$ years each way. Pass out the reproducible on page 74 and get your kids thinking about what they would do on Mars if they were chosen to go.

Sketch a Stamp

In 1997, the U.S. Postal Service issued a Mars Pathfinder postage stamp to commemorate NASA's bold scientific study of Mars. Invite students to design their own postage stamp for a manned mission to Mars (or another mission of their choice) using the reproducible on page 75.

Video Visions of Planets

Let students have a crack at writing their own weather or news report about the planets—and then film them with a video camera. For a backdrop, tape the enclosed planetary poster to the wall. Using the video camera, record students giving a report about any aspect of the planets.

Show What You Know

Reproduce this culminating activity on pages 76–77 and give students a chance to share what they have learned about the planets.

Party on, Planets

Finish your planet unit with a Planet Party and a screening of your students' planet news reports. You'll need planet cookies, a VCR, television, and the "news" videotape. With a few parent volunteers, the party will be a lot of fun for both you and your students.

PLANET COOKIES MATERIALS:

- sugar cookie dough
  (refrigerated prepared dough works well)

- rolling pin

- flour

- colored granulated sugar

- icing (canned icing works well)

- cut out planet shapes from page 23 to help you shape your cookies.

DIRECTIONS:

1 Shape the cookies and bake them according to the package or recipe directions. Let the cookies cool to room temperature.

2 Set the cookies out along with a container of canned icing and dishes of colored sugar. Encourage each student to ice and decorate one cookie to look like his or her favorite planet.

Readers' Theater: **We Are the Planets**

A Magical Tour of the Solar System
By Sandra Bellingham

Characters: (28 total)

- **First Narrator**
- **Second Narrator**
- **Third Narrator**
- **Genie**
- **Sun**
- **Moon**
- **Mercury**
- **Venus**
- **Earth**
- **Mars**
- **Asteroids**
  Three speaking parts
- **Jupiter**
- **Moons of Jupiter**
  Four speaking parts
- **Saturn**
- **Rings of Saturn**
  Six speaking parts
- **Uranus**
- **Neptune**
- **Pluto**

Props:

Cardboard cutouts of Sun, planets, moons, asteroids, and rings, painted by students. These can be attached to painter's sticks so students can hold the cutouts up to their faces.

Hula–Hoops™ can be held by the Rings of Saturn.

First, Second, and Third Narrators come to stage front. Genie waits just offstage. The remaining cast members are on risers or grouped at the rear of the stage. As actors complete their parts, they return to join them.

● ●

First Narrator:
Welcome to our play, *We Are the Planets*. Today, we have an unusual treat in store for you. We're going to take you on a tour of the solar system.

Second Narrator:
Have you ever wished you could just fly out into space and see the Moon, the planets, or even a comet up close? Well, today, with the help of our magical genie, we're going to make your wish come true.

Genie:
(Genie makes a dramatic entrance.)
Hello! I am a genie, and I'd like to grant your wish. But take all of you on a tour of the solar system? I'm afraid I can't do that. You humans have made a big enough mess of things here on Earth. Until you clean it up, you're grounded!

Third Narrator:
But Genie, most of us here recycle, and we try to ride our bikes and walk instead of having our parents drive us everywhere in a car. And we never let the water run when we brush our teeth!

Genie:

Really? Hmmm. *(Puts chin in hand, as if considering)* Well, maybe I can make a little exception in your case. I'll be your guide to the solar system.

All the Cast:

Hooray!

Genie:

Now everyone, come with me. The wonders of the solar system await!

Lights go dim. Earth, with the Moon circling around it, comes to center stage. Sun stands at one end. Narrators and Genie remain onstage. Lights go up.

First Narrator:

Wow! It's so beautiful and peaceful out here. All these beautiful stars and planets are moving in perfect order.

Genie:

There is order, all right. But things do happen out here, and they're not always written in the plan. Come on! Let's go talk to the Moon. The Moon can tell you about some of the exciting things that happen out here in space.

Moon:

Hello, earthlings. I'm the Moon. Earth is my best friend in the whole universe. We're kind of like twins—not identical, of course, since I'm much smaller.

Earth:

Moon and I are sometimes called a twin planet system.

Moon:

That's right. Earth and I used to be much closer. But my, how things have changed.... About 400 million years ago, I circled Earth 13 times a year instead of 12 like I do now.

Earth:

And my days were shorter then, just 22 hours long instead of 24 hours.

Genie:

See? What did I tell you? Space is full of changes.

Moon:

And all this change is my fault. You see, my gravity pulls *(Moon leans away from Earth, and Earth leans toward Moon.)* on the oceans of Earth, gradually slowing the Earth's rotation.

Earth:

Don't forget to tell them what *my* gravity does to *you.*

Moon:

Right! Because of the way Earth's gravity affects my rotation, I move a little farther away from the Earth every year. A long time from now, Earth's gravity just won't be strong enough to hold me. I'll break out of orbit and then it's good-bye. *(Moon looks sad.)*

Second Narrator:

I hope that isn't going to happen in our lifetime!

Genie:

Don't worry! It won't.

Sun enters. Mercury enters, jogging around Sun. Earth and Moon exit.

Genie:

Hey, wait up there, Mercury!

Mercury:

(Pausing, but jogging in place to give impression of hurry and impatience.) Hello. Make it fast. I gotta run. *(Panting)* I go clear around the Sun in 88 days. You people on Earth take 365 days. I'm not only fast, I'm small, too—the second smallest planet in the solar system.

Third Narrator:

Wow! I'll bet we can't even see you from Earth if you're that small and fast.

Mercury:

(Stops jogging to speak lines.) Actually, I've been famous on Earth for more than 5,000 years. The ancient Greeks used to see me in the morning. They called me Apollo, after their god of music and poetry. *(Wipes imaginary sweat from brow.)*

Third Narrator:
How nice. Mercury, are you Okay? You're sweating.

Sun:
Oh, Mercury will be fine. It's my closest neighbor, so I keep it nice and hot: 800 degrees Fahrenheit on the sunny side, 300 degrees in the shade!

Third Narrator:
Wow, now that's hot.

Mercury:
Gotta run. See you!

Mercury jogs offstage.
Sun exits stage.
Venus enters, graceful and haughty.

Venus:
People of Earth, I am Venus, named for the goddess of love. You must not listen to that silly Mercury. He is only a messenger announcing my approach. Of course, you may not want to visit me. My surface is as hot as Mercury's, and my atmosphere is made of sulfuric acid and carbon dioxide. *(Coughs)* I don't have a moon the way Earth does. But why should I? I am perfect the way I am, am I not?

First Narrator:
I think you are!

Venus bows and exits stage.

First Narrator:
Genie, I understand that a lot is happening out here in space. But it sure looks peaceful.

Mars:
(Entering stage front and speaking in agitated voice.) We are peaceful out here in space! What's the worst that happens out here? An escaping comet? A couple of colliding asteroids? Now, on the other hand, you people on Earth...

Genie:
Hey, Mars. Calm down! *(Aside to audience)* Boy, is he a planet with an attitude or what?

Mars:
Well, I'm just sick and tired of being named for the Roman god of war. The only place I know where war happens is Earth. And you point the finger at me!

First Narrator:
Please don't be upset, Mars. We're sorry you don't like the name our ancestors gave you thousands of years ago. You are Earth's nearest neighbor.

Mars:
(Calming down) You're right. We are neighbors, and neighbors should be friends. Actually, now that you are sending spacecraft to explore my surface, maybe we'll get to know one another a little better. Bye!

Mars exits. Entering stage are the Asteroids in something like a conga line, but thumping and jostling each other in a rather ungraceful manner.

First Asteroid:
Hi! We're the Asteroid Belt. We are found in the space between Mars and Jupiter.

Second Asteroid:
We were supposed to turn into a real planet, way back in the beginning of the solar system.

Third Asteroid:
The trouble is, Jupiter and Mars formed first. Their gravity pulled so hard that all our bits and pieces couldn't pull together.

Asteroids jostle one another offstage. Jupiter enters, with several moons slowly orbiting.

Jupiter:
I am Jupiter, named for the ruler of all the gods. And these are some of my sixteen moons. I am soooo big...

All the Cast:
How big is he?

First Moon:
He's so big that he's bigger than all the other planets put together. His gravity is 14 times stronger than the gravity of Earth. Why, he's sooo big...

All the Cast:
How big is he?

Third Moon:
He's so big that his gravity attracts many asteroids and comets. Those troublesome space objects are always hitting Jupiter or one of us moons. I guess that's a good thing for you earthlings. If Jupiter didn't attract the comets and asteroids, the space objects might hit your planet.

Fourth Moon:

That's right. Jupiter protects the inner planets—Mercury, Venus, Earth, and Mars. In fact, some scientists think that if it weren't for Jupiter, a giant asteroid would hit Earth every million years.

First Narrator:

Well, thanks, Jupiter. We earthlings owe you one!

Jupiter and its Moons exit. Saturn and its Rings enter stage. Uranus, Neptune, and Pluto also enter, but remain on the side until they speak.

Saturn:

Hello. I am Saturn, one of the most beautiful objects in the sky! I have thousands of rings. But from Earth, you can only see my six main rings. *(Gestures toward rings)* Here, the rings will tell you all about me...

First Ring:

Saturn is named for the Roman god of agriculture. But you couldn't do much farming here. Saturn has no solid surface!

Second Ring:

That's for sure. Saturn is another one of those huge gas planets with lots of gravity.

Third Ring:

Saturn is the second largest planet in the solar system.

Fourth Ring:

Saturn has plenty of moons. More that 20 at last count!

Fifth Ring:

Saturn's moons prove what a dangerous place the solar system can be. One moon, Mimas, barely survived a collision with a speeding space object. Luckily, Mimas survived with just a giant crater on its surface.

Sixth Ring:

Saturn also has the only moon in the whole solar system that has its own atmosphere. That moon is called Titan. It's Saturn's largest moon of all.

Saturn and the Rings exit. Uranus, Neptune, and Pluto walk slowly to center stage, like royalty in procession.

Uranus:

(Speaks majestically)

Greetings, earthlings. It's good to see you way out here—we never get visitors. I am Uranus. I am almost 2 billion miles away from the Sun. It takes me 84 years to circle the Sun. My neighbor, Neptune, and I are the last giant gas giants of the solar system.

Neptune:

And I am Neptune, named for the ancient god of the sea. I am even farther from the Sun than my friend, Uranus, is. Believe it or not, it takes me 165 years to orbit the Sun!

Second Narrator:

Wow, Neptune. That's amazing!

Neptune:

Oh, that's not all. I am home to a giant storm that is bigger than your entire planet! It is called the Great Dark Spot. I also have a cloudy atmosphere and cold temperatures that reach 375 degrees below zero!

Pluto:

Hi there! I'm Pluto. I'm named for the god of the underworld, because I am more distant and more mysterious than all the other planets. It takes me 250 years to orbit the Sun. No one is certain what I am. Am I really a planet, or am I just an asteroid? Perhaps you earthlings *(Points to the audience dramatically)* will be the ones to uncover my true identity.

Uranus, Neptune, and Pluto exit.

First Narrator:

Thank you, Genie, for taking us on a terrific tour of the solar system.

Genie:

It was my pleasure!

Second Narrator:

(To the audience) And thank you for coming with us.

Third Narrator:

Like the planets and the stars, we are all just travelers through time and space. Thank you for sharing this time and space with us!

The End

Rockets Away Pattern

Cut apart the rocket pieces below and tape them together to make your own model rocket. Your teacher has an instruction sheet.

Roll to make cone for top of rocket

Paper tube for body of rocket

Fins

Rocket Assembly Instructions

Five easy steps to make your rocket!

1

Wrap and tape a tube of paper around the film canister. The lid end of the canister goes down!

2

Lid

3

Tape fins to your rocket.

4

Attach the cone to the top of your rocket with tape.

5

Now your rocket is ready for flight.

Making the Cone

1 Overlap the edges to form cone.

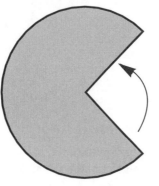

2 Roll a cone of paper and tape it to the rocket's upper end.

NOTE:
NOT TO SCALE.

Name_____

Mission to Mars

Would you like to go to Mars? Only a few lucky astronauts will get to go. The trip will take seven years. You will have to take everything you would need during that time in your spacecraft.

Write NASA and tell them:
- Why you would like to go to Mars
- What you would like to study on Mars
- What you would want to bring with you

Dear NASA:

_____

_____

_____

_____

_____

_____

_____

Sincerely,

_____
Your Name

BONUS:
NASA creates patches to honor every space mission.
Design a patch for your mission to Mars on the other side of this paper.

Name _____

Sketch a Stamp

In 1997, the U.S. Postal Service issued a Mars Pathfinder postage stamp honoring the landing of the Pathfinder on Mars. Design a new postage stamp for the Postal Service that honors a future successful mission landing astronauts on Mars.

PART 1

Name _____

Show What You Know About Planets

Draw features that you can find on rocky planets (Mercury, Venus, Earth, or Mars).

Draw features that you can find on the giant gas planets (Jupiter, Saturn, Uranus, and Neptune).

Name_____

Show What You Know About Planets

Write an **E** next to all the features Earth has.

Make a star ☆ next to all the features Mercury has.

(Circle) all the features Saturn has.

_____ water   _____ rocks   _____ rings

_____ craters   _____ ice   _____ volcanoes

_____ mountains   _____ dust   _____ canyons

_____ moons   _____ clouds   _____ storms

Name that Planet

1._____    2._____

Describe Your Favorite Planet

I like_____   because_____

_____

_____

_____

_____

_____

SUGGESTED CLASSROOM Resources

TEACHER REFERENCE BOOKS

.... *Atlas of Stars and Planets* by Ian Ridpath (Facts on File, 1993)

.... *Merlin's Tour of the Universe* by Neil de Grasse Tyson (Doubleday, 1997)

.... *Rockets: A Teacher's Guide With Activities in Science, Mathematics, and Technology,* NASA publication EG-1996-09-108-HQ

.... *Exploring the Moon: A Teacher's Guide With Activities for Earth and Space Sciences,* NASA publication EG-1997-10-116-HQ

.... *Exploring Meteorite Mysteries: A Teacher's Guide With Activities for Earth and Space Sciences,* NASA publication EG-1997-08-104-HQ

GREAT WEB SITES

.... http://seds.lpl.arizona.edu/nineplanets/

.... http://www.soest.hawaii.edu/PSRdiscoveries/

.... http://www.hq.nasa.gov/education

.... http://spacelink.nasa.gov/

.... http://sse.jpl.nasa.gov/

SLIDE SETS

.... Women in Astronomy (Astronomical Society of the Pacific, 1992)

.... The Lunar and Planetary Institute in Houston has a fantastic planetary slide set. Look for information at http://cass.jsc.nasa.gov/publications/slidesets/

CHILDREN'S BOOKS

.... *Do Stars Have Points?* by Melvin and Gilda Berger (Scholastic, 1998)

.... *The New York Public Library Amazing Space: A Book of Answers for Kids* by Ann-Jeanette Campbell (John Wiley & Sons, Inc., 1997)

.... *The Solar System: Facts and Exploration* by Gregory L. Vogt (Scientific American Sourcebooks, 1995)

.... *Astronomy* by Kristen Lippincott (Dorling Kindersley Limited, 1994)

.... *The Magic School Bus Lost in the Solar System* by Joanna Cole (Scholastic, 1990)

.... *The Day We Walked on the Moon* by George Sullivan (Scholastic, 1990)

.... *The Little Prince* by Antoine De Saint-Exupery (Harcourt Brace Jovanovich, 1961)

.... *Sally Ride: America's First Woman in Space* by S. Blacknall (Dillon Press, 1984)

PICTURES

.... Color images of all the planets can be obtained by contacting NASA CORE, Lorain County Joint Vocational School, 15181 Route 58 South, Oberlin, OH 44074. Phone (440) 774-1051, ext. 249 or 293.

.... *This Dynamic Planet: World Map of Volcanoes, Earthquakes, Impact Craters, and Plate Tectonics.* U.S. Geological Survey map poster, 1994. Reston, VA.

VIDEOS

.... *Planets* - an Eyewitness BBC Scienceworld production, 1997

.... *Volcano* - a National Geographic Society video, 1989

MUSIC

.... "The Planets" by Gustav Holst (many recordings). This classical music suite was based on the astrological and mythological aspects of planets.

.... "Murmurs of Earth" (Warner News Media, 1993). A selection of music from around the world that is traveling on the Voyager spacecraft.

Answer Key

CHAPTER ONE

Tracking Planets (page 24)
answer ..... **Mars should be moving west to east**

What's In a Name? (page 26)
answers .... **Mercury–messenger god; Venus–god of love; Mars–god of war; Jupiter–king of the gods and goddesses; Saturn–god of time**

Poster Activity: Solar System Scavenger Hunt (page 27)
answers .... **1. Jupiter, Saturn, Uranus, or Neptune; 2. Venus; 3. Pluto; 4. Neptune or Pluto; 5. Mercury; 6. Neptune; 7. red; 8. Pluto; 9. Venus; 10. the Sun**

CHAPTER TWO

Comparing Mercury and the Moon (page 41)
Mercury and the Earth's Moon are both round bodies (with a hot side and a cold side). Both have lots of craters from past meteorite collisions. Neither has an atmosphere.

While they look alike, Mercury and Earth's Moon are very different.

1. **Mercury orbits around the Sun.**
2. **Earth's Moon orbits around the Earth.**
3. **Earth's Moon has been visited by astronauts.**
4. **Mercury is too hot for astronauts to visit.**
5. **Mercury is larger than Earth's mooon.**

CHAPTER THREE

Picture Jupiter (page 51)
answer ..... **Check students' work.**

Comparing Gases (page 56)
answer ..... **1. furnace; 2. balloons, blimps; 3. clouds, fog; 4. fertilizer; 5. batteries**

Calculate Your Weight (page 57)
answer ..... **1. - 3. Answers will depend on students' weights; 4. Jupiter; 5. Pluto**

Great Planetary Graph (page 59)
answer ..... **Check students' work.**

CHAPTER FOUR

Show What You Know About Planets (pages 76-77)
Part 1: Rocky Planets
Rocky planets all have a solid surface and may have craters, valleys, volcanoes, geysers, and mountains. Some have atmospheres.
Gas Planets: Giant gas planets have atmospheres and rings.

Part 2: Features
Mark an "E" by all of the features except for rings. Mark a star by craters, mountains, rock, dust, clouds, and canyons. Circle water, moons, ice, dust, clouds, rings, and storms.
4. **Name the Planet: Saturn, Earth**
5. **Favorite Planet: Answers will vary.**